WINDOWS FOR THE SOUL

Wardell
PUBLICATIONS INC

Windows for the Soul

Ecclesiastic Art Glass at Bovard Studio

Ron Bovard

www.windowsforthesoul.com

The creative work presented in this book is the result of the skill and craftsmanship of the entire team here at Bovard Studio both past and present. I especially would like to acknowledge the contribution of two of our designers, Sandor Feher and Joe McManis, who conceived the design layout for this book and prepared much of the art work for pre-press. I also would like to express my gratitude and appreciation to my publisher and editor. Randy Wardell's sharp pen and keen eye added many improvements to this book.

Bovard Studio's fabulous glass painters and designers are an inspiration to watch. Working with our artists I have gained a personal insight into how the studio system of artists, working in groups, resulted in the flowering of Renaissance art. I want to thank all our highly skilled craftspeople and our administrative staff who have devoted their life to this ancient tradition. They have created new stained glass art and have made a significant contribution to the preservation of our stained glass heritage through the repair and restoration of thousands of windows in religious sanctuaries, courthouses, state capitol buildings, libraries, hospitals, universities, and museums throughout the United States and abroad. Finally, everyone at Bovard Studio would like to express our gratitude and appreciation to our clients for the privilege of creating and preserving their stained glass heritage.

Ron Bovard

ACKNOWLEDGEMENTS

Photo of Ron Bovard on the project site of St. Mary of the Angels Church.

Contents

PUBLISHER
Randy Wardell

GENERAL EDITOR
Carole Wardell

TEXT EDITOR
Randy Wardell

LAYOUT & TYPOGRAPHY
Sandor Feher • Joe McManis • Randy Wardell

PHOTOGRAPHY
Except as noted in the text, the photographs were taken by Bovard Studio Inc personal. Including (in alphabetical order)
• Ron Bovard • Paul Conley • Sandor Feher
• Rene Holmberg • Joe McManis • Mike Swoop •

Cataloging in Publication Data
Bovard, Ron
Windows For The Soul
ISBN 0-919985-32-7
1. Bovard, Ron 2. Glass painting and staining–United States. 3. Christian art and symbolism–United States.
I.Title
NK5398.B68A4 2000   748.5913   C00-931061-4

This book is

THIS BOOK IS the the result of an innate desire to share my art, my craft and some of my spiritual insights and impressions. I share my knowledge on the creation of art, execution of craft and restoration and maintenance of our stained glass heritage, including the design and fabrication of new stained glass windows and information on the maintenance and restoration of historic stained glass windows. In addition you will find a portfolio presenting a cross section of Bovard Studio's stained glass projects.

On the deeper level, through the stories of our clients, I am able to share a few spiritual insights based on my personal experiences and perceptions.

To be human and by living a full life one gains more than knowledge, one gains a certain knowingness from within. I have been blessed with a vocation that allows me to explore and express that inner knowledge every day. This book is part of that expression.

Ron Bovard

INTRODUCTION

Cover photo: Garden of Gethsemane stained glass window plus scenes of artists and craftspeople at work in Bovard Studio and on installation.

Center panel from Madonna and Christ Child window (see full window on page 111).

Wardell
PUBLICATIONS INC

To receive our electronic newsletter or to send suggestions please contact us by EMail at: info@wardellpublications.com or visit or web site at: www.wardellpublications.com

Christ in Gethsemane, window designed for the First Presbyterian Church in DeLand, Florida.

Jesus in the Temple, window designed for the First Presbyterian Church in DeLand, Florida.

The Good Shepherd, window designed for the First Presbyterian Church in DeLand, Florida.

Noah's Ark window designed for the First Presbyterian Church in DeLand, Florida.

Sunday Morning,

SUNDAY MORNING, a youth fidgets in the cold hard pew. He stares off into space as a flickering beam of deep mysterious light penetrates his consciousness. Thoughts of heaven and hell, mixed with flashes of divine illumination, filter through his mind. Momentarily his attention is drawn to the stained glass window of Christ praying in the garden at Gethsemane. The sunlight is transformed as it penetrates the stained glass to heighten the look of fresh innocence and eternal love on the face of Christ.

The young man's attention shifts to the window of Christ as a young boy standing in the temple before his inquisitors. The anguished expressions on the faces of the Rabbis' suggest they are uncertain how to react. Trapped by convention they are left with no alternative except to issue a proclamation of "blasphemy" even as they stare into the eyes of God manifest in Christ.

The Good Shepherd window now petitions the boy in a whole new and different way. He begins to understand that all life is infinitely more valuable than the most precious of diamonds and now with the assistance of sunlight filtered through the colored glass he is able to witness the manifestation of God's eternal love from within the Son of a common carpenter.

And over there near the back of the church, why hadn't he noticed the Noah's Ark window before? Again, as in time immemorial, the seed of faith is planted. Will the ground be fertile or barren? Hope springs eternal as the dove returns to the ark with a sprouted olive branch symbolizing that the love of God shines again on Earth.

For the boy sitting in the pew on this Sunday morning his thoughts are lost in these painted images of God and man. His experience is not about the art of stained glass, rather it is about how the light passes through the glass to transform the images in his minds eye. Ultimately the message will penetrate into the heart and soul of this inquisitive child.

Nativity window from Bovard Studio's standard contemporary full-figure series.

H ope springs eternal as the love of God shines again on Earth. Concentrated drops of mankind's individual love trickle into the ocean of God's love, washing against the shores of time, manifest as pure potential waiting for the bather. - R.B.

Above: Detail of "The Temple Priests" from Tiffany Great Chapel window at Reid Memorial Presbyterian Church, Richmond, Indiana. Restored by Bovard Studio.

Above: Detail of "The young Christ" from Tiffany Great Chapel window at Reid Memorial Presbyterian Church, Richmond, Indiana. Restored by Bovard Studio.

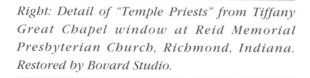

Right: Detail of "Temple Priests" from Tiffany Great Chapel window at Reid Memorial Presbyterian Church, Richmond, Indiana. Restored by Bovard Studio.

As if by mystical intervention he notices one last window. This time he sees the peaceful, loving face and gentle hand of "Christ Knocking at the Door". The choice of eternal life, is the choice of this young boy. Now with fresh eyes and an open heart he gazes unabashedly into the light of the ancient art of stained glass. For the first time in his young life he actually comprehends the spiritual link between his heart, mind and soul as the preacher continues on with Sunday service.

Above and left: The peaceful, loving face and gentle hand of Christ Knocking at the Door. A reproduction in glass of the clients favorite painting. Created for the Berean Assembly of God Church, Des Moines, Iowa.

The love of God is a vast infinite ocean, ever present, omniscient, everywhere. An unhappy person is like a person in the dark, all one has to do is flip on the light switch and enjoy the light. The light switch is the power of our own attention, consciousness itself. - R.B.

Stained glass window at Baker University Chapel in Baldwin, Kansas, restored by Bovard Studio.

Top of page: Bovard Studio 40,000 sq.ft. facilities on 76 acre campus, Fairfield IA.

OVER THE PAST 15 years Bovard Studio has grown from just myself to a staff of over 70 employees. Our artists and craftspeople embody some of the finest talent of our time. Our art department consists of eight glass painters and four designers originating from around the world and our fabricators, restoration staff, and installers have diverse backgrounds and skills as rich and varied as our artists. We truly feel fortunate to have artists from Germany, Hungary, Bulgaria, Ukraine, Canada, Jamaica, and of course most are from the U.S.A.

Prior to establishing Bovard Studio I enjoyed a career as an independent artist for more than 20 years. During that time I was an active member of many artist guilds and trade organizations. Some of my most rewarding experiences occurred when my studio was located in a large warehouse space that accommodated many artists and their studios. The creative camaraderie and cooperative atmosphere was stimulating and I enjoyed working and studying in the company of those artists. However, due to the singular nature of the independent artist most worked alone, producing work exclusive of one another.

At Bovard Studio groups of artists are organized to collaborate and combine forces as a community on all projects. Through this experience I feel I have glimpsed the secret of the Renaissance and its rapid advancement of the arts. I am convinced when groups of artists cooperate and work together every day on project after project, their artistic skills and talents grow and flourish far more rapidly than one would have thought possible when working individually. It has been an amazing inspiration to watch the synergistic growth of our artists.

Much of the success of Bovard Studio's artists can be attributed to the fact that we do not limit our search to experienced glass painters for our art department. In fact glass painting experience is not even considered an asset. Instead we look for talented and creative artists and teach them to paint on glass. When a brilliant artist learns a new medium, the result is brilliant art. It only stands to reason that it is far more difficult, and rare, for a mediocre artist to become a great painter than for a great artist to learn a new medium.

One of the primary motivations behind Bovard Studio's development of our Life of Christ scenes and Religious Symbol Medallion's (see pages 22 to 26), was to create a training program for our new artists to learn and practice the unfamiliar medium of glass painting. They establish their new found skills by painting hundreds of pieces of the same art glass scene. This repetition allows them to master the medium of glass painting in an efficient, economical, and productive way.

Bovard Studio has a number of wholesale distributors that supply a standardized line of hand painted Medallion Scenes to the independent glass studios in the United States, Canada, Europe, Japan, Africa and South America. In addition many of these studios also order custom and original art glass painting directly from Bovard Studio for their religious and other art glass projects.

Many people have asked me how Bovard Studio became so successful in such a short period of time. One major ingredient is that I love my work. For any business to succeed in the long term, you must have a passion what you are doing. Statistics have shown that the success rate for new businesses is very low. Unless you start with outside capital, you may have to work for very little money. Oftentimes, you must pay for the privilege of working in your chosen field for up to three years. This is because most or all of the income generated by the new business must be reinvested back into the business for it to develop and grow. The bottom line is, it's important to select a business you love enough to work at for very little money, often for free, and sometimes at a loss, until you get established. The large majority of new businesses fail within the first three years, so all you may end up with is the joy you had from the effort. As long as you show up and put in a full day's work you are still in business. The longer you do this, the more your chances for success increase.

When I started as an independent artist in 1971, I struggled to make a living as a fine artist, a painter. I had considerable success exhibiting my work in museums and galleries across the U.S. and Europe, including one man shows at some prestigious New York City galleries. I received many approving reviews of my art work in newspapers and magazines and had my work selected for publication in several art books. (See page 157) This was a superb boost for my creative ego but did little to support a growing family which included my loving wife and five children. I managed to sell a substantial amount of art work, but at the end of the year there was far too little difference between the amount of income from gross sales and the expenses incurred to produce those sales.

It took some time for me to recognize that the system is heavily stacked against the artist, as it is in few other businesses. A survey conducted several years ago by the periodical Art Business News, revealed that 90% of the art sold in the United States is categorized as

A rendering for a new window to match the historic style of existing stained glass windows installed in a Catholic church in Indiana.

Easter Lily Window at First United Presbyterian Church.

A new stained glass window by Bovard Studio in the Tiffany plated style for a McLean, Virginia, estate.

Rendering of a standard window theme, Christ with the Children.

"traditional". My circumstantial observation is that the vast majority of artists graduating from art schools in the United States are contemporary artists, yet contemporary art comprises only 10% of the market. To top it all off, I was a contemporary artist.

An additional obstacle is the gallery system. There is huge competition among artists to be exhibited by reputable art galleries through which an artist's work is sold, and his or her reputation is established. The standard practice and requirement for artists is to supply the galleries with their art on a consignment basis. This means the gallery has no financial risk in inventory, leaving the artist to support the gallery with their artwork and assume most of the risk. Many times the artist is expected to pay for other expenses as well, such as framing and some advertising costs. On top of all this, most galleries take 50% to 60% commissions on the gross sale amount of the art. These terms, combined with the overabundance of artists willing to submit to them, have left very few artists in a position to make a reasonable living from their art work.

I had experimented with glass art as early as 1970. In 1982 I took a job as the art director for a company which had developed and patented the process for laser cutting of glass and support systems for abrasive water-jet cutting of glass. It was my duty to develop art and viable products for this new technology to produce. I gained valuable experience working with teams of high caliber engineers developing these technologies for glass cutting. Most of the art work we produced was computer aided design (CAD) which was in very early development at that time. Being no computer whiz I was always selected as the "test dummy" to see if the systems the engineers developed were user friendly.

One of my strengths is that I have always been an enthusiastic individual. My contagious enthusiasm has always helped me to sell my work and selling the new products we developed came naturally to me. As it turned out, I was the most successful sales person in the company. I was continually getting pushed more and more into sales and eventually became the sales manager. The drawback was that I was doing less and less art work and realizing I was no longer doing what I loved to do, I made a decision to move on and resume my career as a full-time fine artist. Fortunately, my compensation at this company included a stock package and I was able to sell my stock to procure enough capital to start over again.

Shortly after I left that company, one of the manufacturer's representatives asked me to develop and manufacture a product line of stained glass for the door and window industry. The idea was to distribute these windows through lumber yard chains and home supply stores. For many months I declined, as my plan was to return to being a fine art painter who also worked in the medium of stained glass.

As fate would have it by January of 1986 I had hit rock bottom financially. The next time this representative called to make the same request again, I said yes. With much urgency in his voice he informed me that he needed the product line developed and the initial stocking order produced and shipped within 30 days. I told him it would take me at least 30 days to raise the capital before I could even start the project. He asked me how much capital I needed, I gave him a number, and the very next morning I received a check from him via Federal Express for the full amount I had quoted. The rest as they say is history and Bovard "Art Glass" Studio was born.

Fortunately I already had a large studio space in an old factory that had been converted into about 30 artist's studios. Having the facilities, I designed the product line, hired several craftspeople, built jigs, set up a production system and shipped out several hundred octagon stained glass window inserts 30 days later.

An example of one of the production window inserts from our product line of "24k gold plated" leaded glass windows we sold through Lowes home supply centers.

I should state at this point that I feel I had an advantage over many people in that I grew up in a family of entrepreneurs. My father had a small business, plus I had uncles and great uncles with small businesses. My wife also grew up in a family of business people. Her father had four businesses during his lifetime, and her maternal grandfather had a very successful large business. So as children both my wife and I witnessed first hand the risks and rewards of business. We lived through the ups and downs, the difficult times, and watched as perseverance turned failures into successes. Both of us were well aware of the swing and cadence of a small business before I started Bovard Studio. A supportive spouse and family is essential in any small business venture because the downs always go along with the ups.

By the end of 1986 we had landed several additional window insert accounts and our production department was in full swing. During that time we continued to develop our custom art glass division and had completed several smaller commissions, but more importantly we successfully completed our first church window commission. Over the next two years our custom business grew and by the end of 1988 it was clear to me that Bovard Studio's future was in architectural and ecclesiastic windows. I made a decision to concentrate our efforts in that direction.

A contemporary design window for Council Bluffs, Iowa Public Library entrance mezzanine.

I wrote to my production stained glass customers and gave them permission to use our copyrighted product lines which we had developed exclusively for them. I included a list of other art glass companies who would be more than happy to accept the accounts. Within a few months we filled our last production orders and we were out of the production business. We were now 100% committed to architectural stained glass. Our target markets would be churches, courthouses, libraries, museums, state government buildings, military bases, restaurants, and hotels. I was exhilarated to be moving forward

Installation view of twelve foot (3.66 m) diameter rose window for Church of the Ascension, Overland Park, Kansas.

into this new phase of business. Architectural glass was the most fulfilling thing I had ever been involved in and I am proud to say that we have been growing ever since.

One of the most important realities an entrepreneur must face is their personal limitation. My experience as a child watching my father and uncles, helped me to see the importance of this lesson early on. So when the circumstance presented itself, I was mentally prepared to hire people who were more talented, with exceptional skills in areas I was lacking. For example our business manager and CFO (chief financial officer) has a strong accounting, banking and small business background with more than 25 years experience. He is one of the smartest businessmen I know. Our production director is a manufacturing engineer with a master's degree in business management with more than 30 years work experience. He is also a gifted Apostolic Catholic priest and bishop. We have several exceptionally talented and gifted artists and designers who run circles around my artistic limitations. Our training instructor for our stained glass fabricators has over 20 years experience and is one of the finest stained glass craftsmen that I know. He is a kind, patient and talented teacher who enthusiastically passes his talents on to new apprentices and helps our experienced craftspeople improve their skills.

I could go on listing the many qualities and special skills each person brings, suffice it to say that every one of our staff members have talents and gifts they bring with them everyday. As a bonus, this group of people are fun to be around. Needless to say, most have many other opportunities to practice their avocation, but they are here at Bovard Studio because they love what they are doing.

Right: A rendering for the rose window shown above installed in Church of the Ascension, Overland Park, Kansas.

THAT LUCKY SOUL whose life was spent in vocation, blissful duty to God, self and mankind is accepting of his fate. Better is life spent performing one's own vocation, no matter how lowly, than in that of another, as that brings great danger to life everlasting. Motherhood, the highest of vocations yet most common, lights the soul of mother. Individual love finds unity in the ocean of God's love. The love of mother for child is the purest of loves. It is love given freely from generation to generation with no expectations, no strings attached. It is mother giving heart, soul, and self, her essential being, pure, focused, concentrated love. This love flowing into baby's heart, nourishes this new life's soul. This love, though only a drop of concentrated individual love, gives us a glimpse of the ocean of God's love, omnipresent, eternal. Unifying bliss, I am That, Thou art That, all of manifest creation is That. All that is lacking are the eyes of the enlightened saved souls to see it. This is pure bliss consciousness, the one true vocation of every man, woman and child blessed with God's highest gift, life as a human being. No drop of precious love is lost as it merges with the ocean of God's love. Love, the treasure of the universe, flows between mother and child, an invincible force of nature, in the highest of holy vocations, motherhood.

A simple mother, Denise of Dallas, Texas, her body filled with cancer, is told by the finest doctors that she is going to die. Time, precious time, has run out. Planning her burial, she pursues one precious thought, her love for her three young daughters. Denise commissions a stained glass window.

Detail of the memorial window showing a guardian angel.

A MOTHER'S LOVE

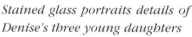

Stained glass portraits details of Denise's three young daughters

Those gifted artists, who are fortunate enough to work in this translucent medium of stained glass share a special knowledge. They understand that it is the light passing through the glass that is the art. Without the light, stained glass is nothing more than a drab and shadowy surface interlaced with a matrix of lead cames. Add the light, and it is possible to see the soul of man shining in the silhouette of God. - R. B.

She plans with Bovard Studio artists a window with her three young daughters playing in the garden. They are swinging among the clouds with their guardian angel's ever protecting conduit of an absent mother's love. The angel hovers over their blissful play, protecting innocent pure hearts, their treasured mother's love an eternal, precious drop in the ocean of God's love.

Defying her doctors', modern day sages, certain predictions, Denise clings to life, waiting the months it takes to see the stained glass window she has commissioned as she painstakingly helps the artists design every detail. In Fairfield, Iowa, Bovard Studio's artists create line by line, glass cut by glass cut, brush stroke by brush stroke, fired indelibly into the stained glass by the tongues of fire in Bovard Studio's gas fired kilns. A glimpse of precious mother's love is captured for time immemorial.

After the final pieces of stained glass are assembled, cradled in their lead cames, Bovard Studio's craftsmen place the final touches on the stained glass in the Dallas mausoleum, Denise's final resting place. Denise arrives with her loving husband and three precious loves. Tears flow freely as she sees her vision is realized. She returns home, to her vocation, a mother's life lived, her soul with all its precious love joins the ocean of God's love.

As we turn around to leave Denise's final resting place, directly across from her memorial stained glass window lies the new grave of Mickey Mantle. Autographed baseballs are piled there by teammates and rivals who stop by to pay their final respects.

When the client-artist trust relationship is in place, artistic license is granted to the artist to make changes and refinements during the process of designing, developing, and building a stained glass window. Often while the glass is being cut or laid out the artist will have an insight for a refinement that will add greater beauty to the finished window. Placing restrictions on this artistic license does not allow for artistic intuition to occur or for artistic genius to manifest itself.

Memorial window for a dying mother, reveals her ascending spirit and a guardian angel keeping watch over her three young daughters. Installed in Hillcrest mausoleum in Dallas, Texas. Artist: Lyn Durham.

It has the power to elevate the humblest church into a temple of God. Stained glass is the "jewel in the crown" of the great cathedrals that have for centuries been the seat of man's search for the kingdom of God within himself. - R. B.

Blessing the Children memorial window incorporating the likenesses of the donor's grandchildren for American Lutheran Church, Jesup, Iowa. Artist: Lyn Durham.

United Presbyterian

Above and Below: Details of medallion scenes for the United Presbyterian Church, Morning Sun, Iowa.

Left: Full window installation showing the placement of a painted medallion scene for the United Presbyterian Church, Morning Sun, Iowa.

United Presbyterian Church, Morning Sun, Iowa

4

*Traditional Apostle
Luke Medallion*

Baptism Medallion

*Traditional Apostle
John Medallion*

HAND-PAINTED MEDALLIONS, BORDERS AND ROSETTES

Stained and decorative glass suffered a steep decline in public interest from the mid 1940's to the early 1960's. The trend in new church buildings was for minimal decoration, with little or no stained glass in the windows. Tiffany lamps had gone out of style and many were thrown out with the trash (those same original Tiffany lamps would now be worth many thousands or even millions of dollars). It became fashionable to use plastics for color and decoration in the home. This was the era when many people decried that stained glass was a dead or dying art form.

The 1960's saw the beginning of a revival for the stained glass craft. The pop culture of the mid 60's exploded onto the scene with it's bold, confident designs and art glass became "cool" to a new generation of Americans. An art medium that used light and color to compose a work of art, was a natural connection to empower the self-expression of the "hip generation".

Custom Design Medallion

Communion Medallion

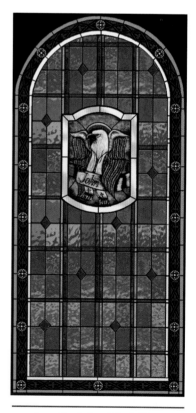

*Apostle John Medallion
shown installed in window*

During the 1970's, proponents and neophyte crafters were attracted to this age-old art form and the revival was truly underway. Small art glass studios were established and artistic experimentation was rampant. Hobby instruction classes were offered everywhere you looked and glass crafting flourished as a do-it-yourself art. New glass manufacturing facilities were born and older established glass factories "rediscovered" lost formulas for making unusual and diverse types of stained glass. It wasn't long before glass, very similar to the type L. C. Tiffany & Co. used at the turn of the century, was readily available.

While there were hundreds of studios now at work producing beautiful stained glass works, one aspect of the art, painting on glass, was trailing behind the progress made in the art glass craft as a whole. Most studios developed and refined their skills as stained glass artists but did not include glass painting in their repertories. Perhaps this was due to a lack of qualified instruction or to difficulty in obtaining the specialized stains and other supplies. Whatever the reason, the scarcity of glass painters turned out to be a golden opportunity for Bovard Studio.

In the late 1990's we recognized there was a need for ready-made glass components with traditional hand-painted motifs, which could be incorporated into stained glass windows. We developed several prototypes of glass medallions, featuring both religious and secular painted designs and made a presentation to one of our trusted suppliers. We showed them our samples and explained the concept of offering authentic hand-painted stained glass medallions to the rapidly growing number of professional and hobby-craft artisans. To our delight, the distributor said yes and we left with a purchase order. Our elegant hand-painted glass products are now carried by most art glass distributors and are available through thousands of stained glass retailer supply stores around the world.

*Traditional St. Michael
Medallion*

*Traditional Apostle
Mark Medallion*

Bible & Cross Medallion

Vine & Branches Medallion

Jesus Knocking - with an optional painted border cluster set.

Blessing the Children

Ascension

Baptism

Resurrection at the Tomb

Madonna and Child

Jesus Walking on the Water

The Good Shepherd

Gethsemane

Bovard Studio's custom medallions include eighteen hand-painted and kiln-fired "Life of Christ" and "Old Testament" scenes. These Medallions are available in 18" x 24" (45.7 x 61 cm) oval, 18" x 24" (45.7 x 61 cm) rectangle and 18" x 24" (45.7 x 61 cm) royal arch shapes. Also available are 12" x 16" (30.5 x 40.6 cm) oval, 12" x 16" (30.5 x 40.6 cm) rectangle and 12" x 16" (30.5 x 40.6 cm) royal arch shapes, along with 9" and 12" (22.8 & 30.5 cm) circles (disk shape). These medallions look great with a simple border added to hang as an autonomous panel or

Nativity

Feeding the Multitude

The Last Supper

Head of Christ

Crucifixion

Annunciation

The Ten Commandments

Daniel and the Lions

Noah and the Ark

they can be incorporated into full-size, custom designed leaded glass windows with borders and a geometric background. See examples on pages 21, 22 & 27 and in the Design Archive chapter 20.

BORDERS

Border components with floral & fauna motifs

BORDERS AND ROSETTES are painted with tracing black pigment that is kiln-fired onto a colored background glass. These components were used extensively in older liturgical and domestic stained glass windows and continue to be used for many traditional designs today. The pattern repeats and matches as it traces around the perimeter of the window. The rosettes are used to anchor the corners or may be interlaced into the border depending on the artist's concept.

The Life of Christ windows on pages 8, 56 & 57 are fine examples of how these components may be used in a stained glass window design.

Border components with geometric motifs

ROSETTES

Rosette components with floral and geometric motifs

These hand painted Borders & Rosettes along with our Medallion Symbol series are available worldwide from many fine retail distributors. For information on availability of these components in your area please log onto our web site at:

www.windowsforthesoul.com

Left: New building addition showing the location of stained glass windows commissioned by The Sacred Heart Church, Bolder Colorado.

New stained glass windows using hand painted medallions were custom designed to compliment existing windows for The Sacred Heart Church in Bolder Colorado.

The Descending Dove (above right) is a standard medallion design. Christ Carried to the Tomb (above) is a custom medallion created especially for The Sacred Heart Church in Bolder Colorado.

5

GOD'S TEST OF FAITH

A window from the United Methodist Church, Hamilton, Illinois after modification, restoration and installation into the new church.

DEEP RUMBLING thunder shakes the ancient bedrock under the new brick building of the United Methodist Church in Hamilton, Illinois. Lightning illuminates the dark evening sky as primal forces rain water and fire down upon the earth. In a sudden flash, bricks fly and timbers burst into flames. This night is to become another one of God's challenges, a test of faith for this young congregation.

Church members and neighbors are instantaneously roused from their homes and without hesitation spring into action. Men and women rush into the burning building, some rescue the new organ from the flames while others recover the pews, setting them safely into the wet grass a safe distance away. A few of the faithful climb upon the over-heated brick walls, rushing trust before personal safety and pull each and every stained glass window from the burning building. Newspaper records of the incident from 1905 reported that "hot molten lead dripped down arms of rescuers, searing their flesh".

This Methodist congregation was first organized in 1853 on the east bank of the mighty Mississippi River just south of Navoo. On this day in 1905 the Methodist faithful are simultaneously devastated and blessed in God's firm hands, symbolized by their newly tempered souls standing before the smoldering embers of the now destroyed 4 year old brick church building. A new challenge has arrived for the forever faithful and like the

Members of the church risked their lives to save the glass from the heat of the flames. A newspaper story preserved from that period reports that hot lead ran down the arms of rescuers who retrieved all windows intact. One can easily surmise that of utmost importance in the construction of our new facility was the continued use of the stained glass windows. - Excerpt of letter from Pastor Paul Smit, Hamilton United Methodist Church, Hamilton, Illinois.

The entrance lobby at United Methodist Church showing how some of the modified windows were incorporated into the new building.

Phoenix this church shall rise again. It was rebuilt in 1910 on the same foundation of the recently destroyed church and the courageously rescued stained glass windows would be incorporated into the new church building.

Time passes along as surely as the ever-flowing Mississippi. By 1987, old age has beset this once proud building. The practical 1980's...what to do? The cost of utilities, maintenance and repair exceeds the cost of a mortgage on a new building that would better serve the needs of today's congregation.

The decision is made to build a new modern church. Money is raised and plans are set but not before the heritage of their ancestors is taken to heart. Those stained glass windows, saved so many years ago by faithful souls must not be cast aside. Could they be redesigned and incorporated into the new building? With the help of Bovard Studio, their precious heritage now rests in the restored stained glass windows that will easily last another 100 years and beyond.

One unique feature of our old building was that every window was stained glass. Along with the beauty the windows provided, was a heritage that gave the glass even greater value. In the early 1900's the church burned shortly after the initial construction was completed. - Excerpt of letter from Pastor Paul Smit, Hamilton United Methodist Church.

Above: This chapel window from Trinity Cathedral in Davenport, Iowa, incorporates salvaged stained glass sections into a simple diamond background.

Right two photos: Salvaged fragments from an old English window prior to cleaning and restoration. These have been incorporated into the new chapel windows (shown above and on page 59) at Trinity Episcopal Cathedral in Davenport, Iowa.

Craft, the hand of God expressed through the hand of man. Stained glass, the medium of God's light perceived through the eye of man. Manifest expression of the unmanifest, the goal of all art at its highest. - R. B.

Above: Window for St. Peter's Episcopal Church, Lake Mary, Florida.

Below: Rendering of a modern design with the Alpha & Omega symbols in a grid background.

WEST ANGELES CATHEDRAL PROJECT

The south central district of Los Angles California is a community on the move. Bishop Charles Blake along with his supportive wife Mae and dynamic congregation are revitalizing a neighborhood that is notorious for its riots, gangs and drive-by shootings. So miraculous is the effect of God's extraordinary passion flowing into this community that it has become a shining example to people everywhere of what divinely inspired men and women of the spirit can achieve. The tide has turned.

In 1969, The (then) Reverend Charles Blake was called to become the pastor of a divided 50-member congregation at West Angeles Church. Unknown to Reverend Blake the congregation had voted, before they had met him, to reject the proposal for him to become pastor of their church, and even after his appointment, there was a movement stirring to exclude him from the church building and grounds. In the midst of this turbulent beginning, Reverend Blake was re-energized through divine intervention and he knew this calling truly was God's plan for his life. Heart, mind, body and soul, plus his absolute rock-solid faith, became the cornerstone for the revitalization of this community.

The central panel on a 108' (32.9 m) high tower of the "Holy Spirit" final selected design.

Rendering of the final selected "Holy Spirit" design for West Angeles Cathedral, shown here as viewed from the interior.

Collage of renderings showing several exterior views and window details for West Angeles Cathedral's Holy Spirit window design in Los Angeles, California.

Above and below: Two concept versions for the West Angeles Cathedral project.

Twenty years later the congregation now numbers 18,000 strong and has over 80 social ministries available to both members and non-members. These ministries include marriage counseling, AIDS support groups, substance abuse recovery, Los Angeles' largest literary program, a prison ministry, a school mediation program aimed at preventing violence, a homeless ministry that feeds 2,000 people a week, and a community development program that has built over 150 low-income housing units (with more underway). The education and training ministries include a Performing Arts Theatre, the School of Success, a Bible College, the School of Practical Christian Living, the School of Leadership Enhancement and Development, and The West Angeles Christian Academy with over 1,600 children in grades K-8. By all accounts West Angeles Church lives up to its statement of affirmation, "Our Children, Our Future."

West Angeles has become the spiritual, social and economic center of south central Los Angeles. Its congregation includes everyone from the impoverished to wealthy business leaders. On any given day you will find single mothers, AIDS sufferers, drug and alcohol abuse victims, worshiping alongside trend setting movie stars, distinguished

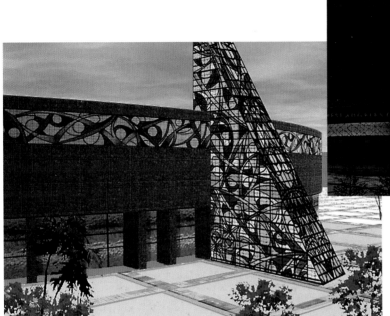

Two concept versions for the West Angeles Cathedral project.

professional athletes, and community leaders. The co-chairmen of West Angeles Cathedral's building committee are Denzel Washington and Magic Johnson. They, along with the entire congregation, have raised funds to build a 5,000 seat cathedral that is far more precious than its framework of steel and exterior covering of Karelian granite and stained glass curtain walls. It truly is a beacon to the soul of man.

The West Angeles Cathedral under construction in Spring of 2000, Los Angeles, California.

West Angeles Cathedral

Above 3 images: Concept proposals for the West Angeles Cathedral project. Background: Detail from blueprint of new cathedral building.

When Reverend, now Bishop Blake and Mrs. Blake visited our studio in Fairfield, Iowa, to consult on the design for West Angeles Cathedral's stained glass, our entire staff was struck by their powerful spiritual light. We experienced that same spiritual presence of God that is revitalizing south central Los Angeles. Whether Bishop Blake is preaching to 150,000 believers in Uhuru National Park in Nairobi, Kenya, to a conference of 100,000 Pentecostal ministers and delegates gathered in Seoul, South Korea, or to his home congregation in Los Angeles, California, there can be no doubt that darkness has been overpowered by the light.

Above: A conceptual rendering of an interior view depicting the colorful "Holy Spirit" theme that the client's selected as the final design for West Angeles Cathedral project.

Above and right: Two different concept proposals for window walls at West Angeles Cathedral.

7

CREATING STAINED GLASS WINDOWS - AN OVERVIEW

DESIGN DEVELOPMENT

The first step in creating a stained glass window is to determine the desire of the church congregation, usually through consultation with an art window committee. It is the designer's task to interpret the clients desire for expression of faith, history, or aspirations within the chosen artistic style. They will set aside sufficient time to discuss the project in detail, exchanging ideas using photographs, drawings, and sketches until a concept is revealed. The designer will then prepare a color proposal rendering for presentation, after which refinements will be made until a final design is agreed upon.

GLASS SELECTION

One of the most significant stages in the creation of a stained glass window is glass selection. There are literally thousands of different colors, textures and densities of glass available today. The designer will propose a selection of glass for the various areas of the window coinciding with the final color rendering and together with the client, make the final decisions for the colors and textures from actual glass samples.

GLASS PAINTING

Not all stained glass windows have painted details. Depending on the design style chosen, a window may require painting to define border and/or background details. If the design is figurative, painting will be necessary to add realistic details to the faces, hands, and clothing. After the glass has been cut and shaped into the various component pieces, the artist applies the paint, using traditional glass "stains", mat blending colors, and colored enamels. This process of "staining" the glass is where the term "stained glass" comes from.

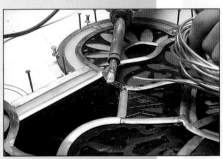

ASSEMBLY AND FABRICATION

After every glass component has been cut, shaped, and painted it is time to assemble or "lead up" the stained glass window. Usually the designer will make one final inspection of the window arranged on a light table or glass easel to view it exactly as it will be assembled. Once satisfied, the fabricator begins the leading process by stretching an "H" channel strip of lead (called a "came") then place it on the assembly drawing along one outside edge of the window. The first glass piece is positioned and temporarily held with a tack nail. Another lead strip is cut, shaped and positioned then the second, adjoining glass piece is arranged into the assembly. This operation continues until every component is in place. The final step in the assembly process is to solder the lead strips together at each joint, to hold the stained glass window together.

CEMENTING AND CLEANING

This important process will stiffen and strengthen the leaded panels, making them weather tight. The cement or putty is pushed into the space between the flanges of the lead came and the glass, on both sides of the window. Then the excess is cleaned off with a special compound called "whiting", leaving the glass unsoiled and imparting an aesthetically pleasing dark "patina" on the surface of the lead came.

INSTALLATION

When the window is complete, the client will be contacted to set an appointment for installation of the new stained glass window. This is a crucial final step and it must be performed by qualified installers who understand the requirements for reinforcing. If exterior protective glazing was specified for the window, it should be installed at this time as well.

CREATING STAINED GLASS WINDOWS - AN OVERVIEW

8

DESIGN DEVELOPMENT PROCESS

WHEN A CLIENT wants a new stained glass window, the first and most important step is to listen carefully to the client's request. Of course, we must also consider the architectural space, adjoining windows, building style, light source intensity and direction, and any trees, buildings, mountains, or other obstacles that may block the available light. All these variables must be taken into account during the process of forming the core concept but in the end, it all comes down to fulfilling the client's desire.

Left: New windows being designed by Sandor Feher using a computer to create a 3-D simulation of the finished art glass as it would look in the building after installation.

In the not too distant past we would render our design proposal as a watercolor painting or use colored dyes on transparent film to illustrate our concept for the client's approval. Today we create our proposal rendering using our computer aided design (CAD) system. It takes our artists about the same length of time to create a digital rendering as it did to produce a watercolor painting. However with a digital design, we don't have to start over if the client wants to make changes. Now changes to the proposal, even major ones, such as a complete color makeover or a proportion adjustment are made quickly and simply, allowing us to communicate with our client graphically in a way they can understand. It is our responsibility to demystify the process for them.

A proposal rendering created with a computer aided design (CAD) system for a Georgia Performing Art Center.The 3-D views of the proposal renderings show how they would appear after installation into the building.

Transmitted Light

An easy way to experience the contrast of transmitted light is to look at a familiar church window from the outside during the day, you'll notice a very dramatic difference.

The client may also need some guidance to help them understand the unique nature of stained glass as a "transmitted light" medium. If you look at a stained glass window in reflected light, (from the same side as the light source) you will find yourself looking at a relatively dark surface, with a few light colored opalescent (milky) glass areas. An easy way to experience this is to look at a familiar church window from the outside during the day, you'll notice a dramatic difference. Even the opalescent glass areas have a very different, less interesting characteristic in reflected light.

The same window as on the right viewed from the outside during daylight in "reflected light". The contrast is dramatic.

Above is an example of an interior "transmitted light" view. Good Shepherd window installed in United Presbyterian Church of Morning Sun, Iowa.

This brings us back to the rendering. A proposal rendered on paper, by its very nature, is presented in a medium of reflected light. At best, it can only give the client an indication of how the finished stained glass will look. Even a proposal prepared on transparent film, which is a medium of transmitted light (similar to stained glass), cannot portray the depth and richness of stained glass. Very few clients are able to visualize the overall effect of the glass in the finished window even when colored glass samples are presented along with the rendering. For this reason, it is very important to establish a trust relationship between the client and the stained glass artist.

The most innovative and poetic work is accomplished by allowing an experienced artist the creative freedom to visualize. Of course they must stay within the clients established design boundaries as well as other considerations such as correctness of religious symbols, liturgy, architectural styles, and artistic style factors such as modern, traditional, abstract, representational, etc.

T he most innovative and poetic work is accomplished by allowing an experienced artist the creative freedom to visualize.

A computer rendering that has been approved by the customer (notice signature in lower right). This color image will serve as a guide throughout the production of the window.

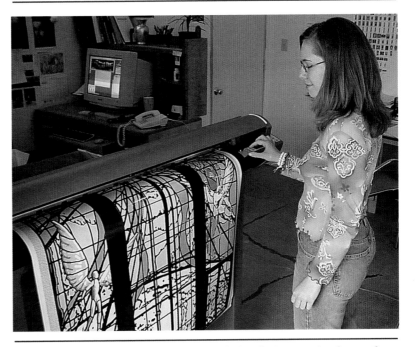

Ron's daughter Tess Bovard, one of the designers, is shown here printing a poster sized proposal on the ENCAD system color plotter.

GLASS SELECTION AND FABRICATION

Top: Laying out the lead lines of a pattern using a computer. Above: Shawn Robinson is printing a full-size pattern from the computer on a pen plotter.

When the client and artist have settled on a design, the project is scheduled and full-size measurements and templates are taken. The artist begins by drafting a full-size pattern drawing consisting of the lead lines in the window.

Lead is the matrix that holds the dozens, hundreds or even thousands of colored glass pieces together in the finished window. A "leaded" glass window is fabricated using lead strips (called "cames") that are extruded in the shape of an "H". A window may use only one size of came or it may have several sizes and shapes to fulfill certain design effects. Artistically the lead lines create a negative space (areas not transmitting light) and the careful mix of negative and positive space is very important in any work of art.

Structural composition is the rudimentary element that determines how long a stained glass window will last. A large window will be fabricated in several independent sections that will be layered or stacked during installation into the window frame. Leaded glass windows should be limited to panel sections of 12 square feet (1.2 m^2) or less. A competent designer must take into account the structural requirements for the chosen design and make the necessary adjustments based on the window's proportions. If designed, fabricated and installed correctly a stained glass window will last for generations.

Man has the power to create his own reality through the power of his consciousness. He can choose to live in the ever changing desert of temporal pleasures and suffering. If we simply go to The Kingdom of God within us all, we can connect to a pipeline that is ever flowing from the ocean of God's love. Quenching the desert of temporal existence to make it bloom in spiritual bliss. - R. B.

Left: A "leaded" glass window is fabricated using lead strips (called "cames") that are extruded in the shape of an "H".

GLASS SELECTION

One of the most significant stages in the creation of a stained glass window is glass selection. We literally have thousands, close to 4,000 different colors, textures and densities of glass readily available today. The various types of stained glass range from clear "cathedral" or semi see-through colored glass to "opalescent" or milky (white-streaky) glass. It may be manufactured or "rolled" by machine or it may be hand-mixed and rolled by a small crew of glassmakers. Alternatively, it may be made mouth-blown by skilled artisans in the "antique" tradition. The varieties of glass you may encounter within these manufactured types are seedy (bubbles), crackle, flashed, reamy, and streaky glass. You will also find a variety of textures available such as ripple, baroque, granite, water, fibrillated, chipped, and many others.

To expand the available range of color, texture and density even further, American artists such as Louis Comfort Tiffany and John LaFarge devised a process called "plating" which they used extensively in their stained glass windows. A "plate" is a second layer of glass, added to a selected area within the window to create a new color or to increase the perception of depth. Some art glass windows fabricated by the L.C. Tiffany & Co. in the late 1800's & early 1900's have areas with up to seven plates on top of one another to achieve the artists desired effect.

Just imagine, we have an assortment of more than 4,000 glass varieties available to us and placing two layers together theoretically expands the glass selection possibilities to a mind numbing 16,000,000. Those possibilities expand exponentially as more plate-layers are added. Of course, with each subsequent layer of plating, the glass density increases thereby lowering the transmitted light, so limitations do exist.

The various types of stained glass range from clear "cathedral" or semi see-through colored glass to "opalescent" or milky (white-streaky) glass.

A careful examination of this photo of a restored Tiffany window reveals extensive use of plating. The arrows on the photo point out some of the multi-level plated areas.

We literally have thousands, close to 4,000 different colors, textures and densities of glass readily available today.

Glass Cutting

Artist Lyn Durham making refinements and adjustments as the glass is cut and laid out on the pattern and set on the light table.

The glass pieces are cut out, painted and waxed up on a glass easel or laid out on a light table to check the effect of light passing through the stained glass composition. Example shown is St. Boniface window for Christ the King Abbey, Cullman, Alabama.

GLASS CUTTING AND SHAPING

Once the glass selection has been finalized and the full-size drawing is complete, it is time to select the actual glass sheets that will be cut into the component pieces for the window's design. The artist must carefully choose the ideal area of the colored glass sheet, taking into account the variations within the sheet, to achieve the desired artistic expression. As pieces are cut they are laid out on a light table, or a viewing easel. The easel is a sheet of clear glass that is positioned in front of a natural light window and the stained glass pieces are temporarily fixed onto it.using sticky wax. This way the artist can examine the effect of light passing through the stained glass composition. They will examine color, density, streak direction, texture, and any other aspect that may have an effect on the overall composition and make refinements and adjustments as necessary. When the client-artist trust relationship is in place, artistic license is granted to the artist to make changes and refinements during the process of designing, developing, and building a stained glass window. Often while the glass is being cut or laid out the artist will have an insight for a refinement that will add greater beauty to the finished window. Placing restrictions on this artistic license does not allow for artistic intuition to occur or for artistic genius to manifest itself.

GLASS PAINTING

While not all stained glass windows have painted details, a large percentage of ecclesiastic window designs do require some painting to define border and/or background details. Figurative designs require painting to add realistic details to faces, hands, feet, and to enhance the clothing. After the glass has been cut and shaped into the various component pieces, the artist applies the paint, using traditional glass "stains", mat blending colors, and/or enamels. Most glass "stains" are made from metal oxides. For instance gold oxide will produce a red color, silver oxide produces yellow or gold, and cobalt yields a blue color. Many different oxides and paints are used to "stain the glass", depending on the desired color or effect.

The artist mixes the glass paints in medium such as water, alcohol or oil, and may additionally include a binder, glass frit and/or paint flux depending on the formula for that particular stain. The artist laboriously grinds and mixes these components by hand with a muller or a palette knife until they have achieved the desired consistency.

Gold oxide will produce a red color, silver oxide produces yellow or gold, and cobalt yields a blue color; almost any metal oxide can be used to stain the glass, depending on the desired color or effect. As an interesting side note, this process of "staining" the glass is where the term "stained glass" comes from.

Rose Buford, one of Bovard Studio's glass painters is seen here working on custom figure medallions.

Artist Ginny Sorak is creating a memorial window with realistic portraits of five martyred Nuns.

After the paint has been applied, artist Ilie Honkaen places the glass in a kiln to be "fired" and permanently bond the paint to the surface of the glass.

When painting a figurative piece, the first layer of paint consists of the tracing lines, usually black, applied with a sable "tracing" brush. After the tracing lines have been applied, the glass is "fired" in a kiln to permanently bond the paint to the surface of the glass. The next paint layer is called a mat (or matting) that requires a special blending brush hand-made from English badger hair. This light brownish mat paint is applied as a fine layer then blended with the badger brush to make it uniform and semi transparent. Once air-dried, this mat layer will be carefully brushed away (called lighting) by the artist to expose the areas that are to remain transparent. This stage of glass painting is the opposite of most painting practices. In this instance, the image is formed by lifting the paint off the matted surface of the glass. This matting process may be repeated a number of times, layering more mats over the first to create artistic depth and differentiation. Once the mat is to the artists satisfaction the glass is placed back into the kiln for a second firing to bond the mat layer to the glass surface. Depending on the design, there may be one or more final painting steps to apply more mats, opaque colors, additional stains or transparent enamels to the image. It will then be finished with one last kiln firing. A special note about kiln firing, the glass may be fired after each painting stage or it may be fired once with multiple layers of paint depending upon the artist's selected technique and preference.

SURFACE ETCHING A DESIGN

Surface etching is another technique that an artist may use to obtain contrasting colors within an individual piece of glass. A special type of glass called "flashed" is used for this process. Flashed glass is manufactured by applying a very thin layer of a darker color onto the surface of a lighter colored sheet of glass. The darker thin layer (the "flashed" layer) can be etched, engraved or sandblasted away to reveal areas of the lighter color underneath in whatever design is desired. For example, an artist may use a blue flashed on clear, then etch a design by removing some of the blue surface color to create a design of clear "stars" on a dark blue "sky" background. We used this technique for the stars in the Garden of Gethsemane window on the front cover of this book.

FINAL INSPECTION

After every glass component has been cut, shaped, painted, etched or otherwise prepared, it is time to assemble or "lead up" the stained glass window. However, not before one final, and very important inspection is made. All finished glass components are arranged back on the light table, or fixed to the viewing easel, exactly as they will be assembled and the artist will make one final review of the work.

Detail of a stained glass window showing an example of symbols etched out of red flashed glass. Detail from a window created for the Veterans' Administration Hospital, Knoxville, Iowa.

ASSEMBLY OR "LEADING-UP" THE WINDOW

Now the fabrication craftsperson takes over to assemble the stained glass window. The glass components are placed on the assembly bench and arranged on the working drawing according to the pattern lines.

The fabricator starts in one corner of the window and begins the leading process by stretching an "H" channel of lead came and placing one strip on the drawing along the bottom and another strip along one side of the window. The first glass piece (usually a corner piece) is placed in this perimeter channel and temporarily held with a tack nail. Another piece of H lead is cut to size with a sharp lead knife or diagonal nipper pliers (called dykes) and shaped to fit around the exposed edge of the first glass piece.

A second, adjoining glass piece is placed in the perimeter channel and another lead strip is cut and placed along the exposed glass edge of that piece. This process continues along, placing glass, cutting and fitting lead strips, until every component is in place. The final step in the leading process is to solder the lead strips together at each joint creating one continuous metal matrix to hold the stained glass window together. The window is then turned over and soldered on the backside. Depending on the size of the window and the skill of the fabricator, the leading and soldering process could take hours or even days to complete.

Modern lead came is extruded from a lead alloy which uses additives to enhance the tensile strength. Older lead came (and some still available) was made from pure lead through a milling process that stresses the came and shortens its life expectancy.

Left: A fabricator cuts H lead came to size with a lead knife and above Llona Wagner is shaping the came to fit around the exposed edge of the glass pieces which are temporarily held in place with a push pin.

Kris Lambert uses a brush to fill the space between the flange of the lead came and glass with glazing cement. This process stiffens the stained glass window and makes it weather tight.

CEMENTING AND CLEANING

The assembled window is now ready to be cemented. This important process will stiffen and strengthen the leaded panels, making them weather tight, and adding an aesthetically pleasing dark "patina" to the lead surface. The cement or putty is pushed into the space between the flanges of the lead came and the glass on both sides of the window, then the excess is cleaned off with a compound called "whiting". The whiting also polishes and cleans the glass surface. There is division among stained glass professionals on the best formula for glazing cement. Primarily if a hardener (such as plaster) should be added to the glazing formula, or if an unaltered commercially produced linseed oil based glazing putty is best. Our experience is that if a protective exterior covering is part of the final installation, simple linseed oil putty without hardener is adequate. However, if no protective covering is to be used, we have found that a cement containing plaster results in a stiffer, more solid panel that is less prone to water leakage, especially in wind-driven rain.

The excess cement is cleaned off with a compound called "whiting" which also polishes and cleans the glass surface.

Some cementing compounds have a black dye component added to enhance the new "silvery colored" lead with a dark, richly colored patina on the surface of the came to give it a more mature appearance.

When a client wants a new stained glass window, the first and most important step is to listen carefully to the client's request. Of course, we must consider the architectural space, adjoining windows, building style, light source intensity and direction, plus look for any trees, buildings, mountains, or other obstacles that may block the available light. All these variables must be taken into account during the process of forming the core concept, but in the end, it all comes down to fulfilling the client's desire. - R.B.

Computer rendering for Redland Baptist Church, using a Dove, Cross and Grape Vine design.

Proposal rendering showing two of the fourteen Stations of the Cross for The Assumption of the Blessed Virgin Mary Parish.

10

Structural Reinforcing

Structural Reinforcing

STRUCTURE AND REINFORCING

Above: This view clearly shows how the oversized areas within a window's framework needs to be divided with mullions, muntins, and steel horizontal T-bars.

In an earlier chapter, we discussed the importance of structural composition during the designing process (see page 44). The designer made some calculations and limited the individual sections in the window to 12 square feet (1.2 m²) or less and has made provisions for all other structural requirements based on the window's design and proportion.

Lead is a very soft metal. This softness provides the flexibility that enables the fabricator to easily shape the lead came strips to fit around the curves and bends in the window's design. Unfortunately, the lead

Installation of the massive "Hand of God" window for Maxwell Air Force Base, Montgomery, Alabama.

alone does not possess sufficient tensile strength to hold any substantial weight within the frame on its own. If a stained glass window were fabricated and installed as one large section, the weight of the upper leaded section would press down upon the lower panels causing them to bow and eventually collapse. You often see this occurring in older leaded glass windows. Imagine a set of children's building blocks stacked up. As long as the blocks are stacked up in a perfectly flat vertical plane, they are stable. Once the stack begins to bow, instability increases exponentially with the increasing degree of deflection (bowing and bulging) and they all come tumbling down. The same is true of leaded glass windows.

To minimize this problem, a steel reinforcing system is used to supplement and divide the window frame (and therefore the stained glass window), into several smaller independent sections. These frame dividers are called mullions and usually add a decorative pattern to the window framing in addition to ensuring stability for the leaded glass. Any section or opening within the window's frame that is larger than 12 square feet (1.2 m²), should be further divided with horizontal T-bars (called muntins). These steel or aluminum T-bars are fastened securely to the window's framework. They supplement the mullions, to transfer the weight of the upper leaded glass panels to the window frame, rather than entrusting the lower stained glass panels to support the weight of the upper panels.

In addition to the mullions and muntins breaking the window frame into smaller sections, the leaded glass windows also require supplemental reinforcing. The old-fashioned method of supplemental window reinforcing was to install the leaded window sections then affix horizontal steel bars into the sash of the window frame at 1-1/2 to 2 foot (45.7 to 61 cm) intervals. These steel bars would be on the inside of the stained glass and would be attached to the leaded panel using copper wires that were soldered to the lead came and wrapped around the steel reinforcing bar.

The more modern method of supplemental reinforcing is to use flat steel bar that is 1/8" thick x 1/2" wide (3 mm x 1.3 cm) and is cut slightly longer than the window is wide. This flat bar is set perpendicular (90°) to the glass surface and laid horizontally across the width of panel. The bar is soldered directly to the lead came at any point where they touch. If possible, the bar is centered across the panel at solder joint areas, which provide greater holding strength. To achieve maximum stability it is essential that the ends of the reinforcing bar be firmly attached to the window frame on installation.

A window showing areas of bowing and bulging at the bottom from the weight of the sections above.

Mark Steele soldering steel reinforcing bars to a stained glass panel at the Maxwell Air Force Base Chapel. Eighteen inches (46 cm) is the typical spacing for reinforcing bars. Artistic considerations as well as structural requirements may affect the final placement of the reinforcing bars.

11

As a rule, most stained glass window installations will benefit from an exterior protective covering. An exterior covering reduces air infiltration, improves the security of the building and reduces the likelihood of vandal or storm damage to the window.

PROTECTIVE EXTERIOR COVERING

As a rule, most stained glass window installations will benefit from an exterior protective covering. An exterior covering reduces air infiltration, improves the security of the building and reduces the likelihood of vandal or storm damage to the window.

However, it is of the utmost importance that the exterior glazing be properly installed and ventilated or significant damage to the stained glass window could occur. Unvented protective covering has caused more damage to historic stained glass windows in the U.S.A. than any other factor (see bibliography listing for Inspired Partnerships' study on protective covering). Unvented protective covering causes damage to both the stained glass window and the window's frame in two ways.

First, we have all noticed that in certain weather conditions condensation will collect on the interior surface of a "single layered" glass window. When a protective covering is installed on the exterior of a stained glass window, the condensation will collect on the inside surface of the protective covering. This means that the condensation is occurring in the space between the stained glass window and the protective covering. If this area is not vented to allow the moisture to dry out between condensation cycles, this space stays continuously moist. The dust on the stained glass becomes "hygroscopic" dust, meaning it stays permanently moist, like a wet sponge. Microorganisms grow rapidly in this environment and they secrete acids that attack the lead, the stained glass, and the window frame. This problem does not happen when insulated glass units are used as exterior protective covering.

From our observations while restoring stained glass windows with this type of problem, the lesser the space between the stained glass window and the unvented protective covering, the more severe the damage becomes. The greater the space, the less severe the damage. A quick

Left: This photo shows the location of vent portals in the protective covering to allow condensation moisture to dry out between condensation cycles and to relieve heat buildup. The upper 2 panels show the protective Lexan panels installed prior to removing white paper surface film covering the Lexan.

inspection will give clear evidence if this moisture problem exists. From the outside of the building, look at the surface of the lead behind the single-glazed protective covering. If you detect a white "lead oxide" powder (the equivalent of rust on steel); this window has a problem.

The second problem caused by unvented protective covering is heat build up. Stained glass absorbs much more of the sun's energy than clear window glass. In fact, a dark piece of stained glass can absorb up to 60% of the sun's energy when unvented protective covering is in place. One study, conducted on a sunny January day in Chicago, recorded temperatures in the air space as high as 150°F, when outside temperatures were 20°F. As temperatures change from cold to hot, building materials constantly expand and contract. Severe temperature fluctuations, as indicated in this study, produces unnecessary expansion and contraction cycles and is a major contributor to premature metal fatigue in the lead came that could result in buckling of leaded glass windows.

A properly vented protective covering should be designed and installed by a qualified stained glass professional. The Stained Glass Association of America (SGAA) in Kansas City, Missouri, has published standards for protective glazing installation. (Please refer to the bibliography on page 158 for more information).

This window has a white "lead oxide" powder (the equivalent of rust on steel) on the surface of the lead indicating it had a problem with moisture build-up between the protective covering and the stained glass window.

Right: An engineered protective glazing installation for First United Methodist Church in Iowa City, Iowa. The elaborate glazing process uses aluminum framing material that is custom bent to match the rose window's mullion tracery. The center circle and each petal on the rose design has a new aluminum frame secured to the top of the original wooden frame. Then each section is fitted with laminated glass (double glass with a plastic core). The venting for this installation was accomplished by creating hidden portals strategically located in the bent metal frame.

Creation window for the First Presbyterian Church in DeLand, Florida.

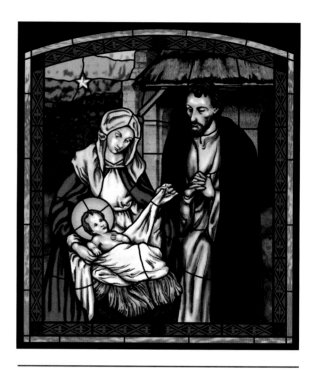

Nativity window for the First Presbyterian Church in DeLand, Florida.

Baptism of Jesus, window for the First Presbyterian Church in DeLand, Florida.

How to respond to this Christ? God manifesting as man on Earth seeing the divine, infinite eternal wisdom, infinite love, absolute truth, ice cold yet unfathomable warmth, perfect, in-your-face love reflected in his eyes seated here and now, right in front of their own eyes, he is frozen in the moment. - R.B.

Crucifixion, window for the First Presbyterian Church in DeLand, Florida.

It is morning, the sun rises and the new morning's light rushes down upon the earth. Nature breaks the new morning's light into a infinite spectrum of colors, densities, and shades, displaying the textures of our world. Artists create stained glass windows to reflect nature's creativity. Churches, Synagogues, and all places of worship stand as the manifest embodiment of generations of spiritual seeker's, their attention on divine joy and spiritual happiness. The morning light streams through the stained glass windows bathing the worshiper in the new morning's light, breaking it into natures diversity of colors, density and shades displaying the textures of our search for God. The faithful seek and they find God. – R. B.

Resurrection, window for the First Presbyterian Church in DeLand, Florida.

Note: Turn to page 8 to see more examples from this "Life of Christ" series windows for the First Presbyterian Church.

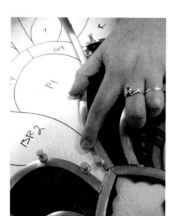

The photograph shows a window being leaded up using extruded "lead alloy" came.

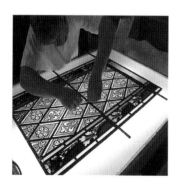

Nick Davis is placing steel reinforcing bars on this window section which will hold the stained glass panel in a flat plane.

ESSENTIAL ELEMENTS of a correctly designed and fabricated leaded glass window.

A professionally designed, structurally fabricated, and properly reinforced leaded glass window will require little or no maintenance for the first 60 to 70 years of its existence. In order for a stained glass window to meet this standard, the following factors must be present:

• The framework of a large window must be subdivided with mullions to create smaller sections. These mullions usually add a decorative pattern to the window framing in addition to ensuring stability for the leaded glass.

• Individual leaded glass panel sections should be 12 square feet (1.2 m²) or less. Any section or opening within the window's frame that is larger than 12 square feet (1.2 m²), should be further divided with horizontal T-bars (called muntins). These steel or aluminum T-bars are fastened securely to the window's framework. They supplement the mullions, to transfer the weight of the upper leaded glass panels to the window frame, rather than entrusting the lower stained glass panels to support the weight of the upper panels.

• Leaded glass designs that have a high number of smaller pieces, or designs that feature concentric geometric patterns, should be smaller than 12 square feet (1.2 m²) per individual section.

• Leaded glass windows must be fabricated with lead came that has sufficient tensile strength. For this reason it is crucial to use a lead came manufactured by the extrusion process using a lead alloy that contains antimony, silver, copper, or tin. Milled came made from pure lead (without alloy additives) is too soft and will not hold up for long, even under normal conditions.

• The leaded glass windows must be properly sealed with a commercial cementing compound or putty that is pressed under the flanges of the lead came. Once the cement has set, it will make the panel more ridged and weather tight.

• In addition to a well engineered matrix of mullions and muntins, leaded panels must have a supplemental reinforcing system. Steel re-bars must be securely soldered or wire tied to the lead came and attached to the window frame. The proper function of a reinforcing bar is to hold the stained glass in a flat plane, it is not to hold the stained glass up. Once the stained glass begins to sag or bulge out of a flat plane it becomes weak and will tend to bulge more and more until the lateral pressure on the glass causes it to break. The smaller the stained glass component parts, the closer the steel reinforcing bars need to be, on average every 18 inches

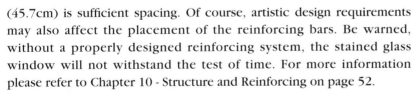

Above: Steel reinforcing bars need to be placed approximately every 18 inches (45.7cm), however, artistic design requirements may also affect the placement of the reinforcing bars. Here we see Mark Steele bending the rebar to follow along a gentle curve in the windows lead design.

Above: Steel reinforcing bars need to be placed approximately every 18 inches (45.7cm), however, artistic design requirements may also affect the placement of the reinforcing bars. Here we see Mark Steele bending the rebar to follow along a gentle curve in the windows lead design.

Left: This chapel window, from Trinity Episcopal Cathedral in Davenport, Iowa, incorporates salvaged stained glass sections into a simple diamond background. Its an excellent example of how mullions are used to break a large window opening into smaller sections. The four large lower sections plus the decorative tracery mullions in the upper section add interest and intrigue to the overall design.

(45.7cm) is sufficient spacing. Of course, artistic design requirements may also affect the placement of the reinforcing bars. Be warned, without a properly designed reinforcing system, the stained glass window will not withstand the test of time. For more information please refer to Chapter 10 - Structure and Reinforcing on page 52.

• If an exterior protective covering is installed it must be properly vented to allow the moisture, that collects in the space between the stained glass window and protective covering, to dry out between condensation cycles. For more information please refer to Chapter 11 – Protective Exterior Covering on page 54.

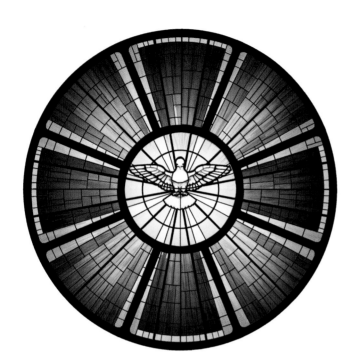

Above: The Rose Window at Christ The King Catholic Church, Ann Arbor MI. Design inspired by a stained glass window in St.Peter's Cathedral, Rome, Italy.

Above & Left: Rendering for St. James Cathedral. To be built by laminating colored art glass to a layer of tempered clear sheet glass.

Above: Computer rendering for Grace Lutheran Church, with biblical quotes on the banners.

Right: Collage of restoration project for the historic Charles Connick stained glass windows at Fourth Presbyterian Church in Chicago, Illinois.

Exterior view of the restored windows installed back into the Chapel's beautifully carved stone frames. Above right: A refined English style garden landscapes the backyard of the Chapel.

T he sanctuary was animated in anticipation of the arrival of the special guest speaker. This individual had spent many Sundays of her youth here, as her father was the Pastor for the congregation at this rural English chapel.

BAKER UNIVERSITY CHAPEL, BALDWIN, KANSAS

An historic English chapel was moved stone by stone from its rural setting in England to the campus of Baker University in Baldwin, Kansas. Now perfectly restored, this beautiful chapel looks as if it had been there from the very beginning. A refined English style garden blends the rear of the Chapel into the surrounding Kansas landscape.

The Chapel windows are exquisite examples of English traditional stained glass design. The greatest responsibility in this restoration project was to find a suitable replacement glass and to recreate the painted details for the broken and missing components damaged in handling and transport from England to Kansas. The client challenged our artists to produce replacement pieces that were indistinguishable from the original.

We completed the restoration and installed the windows back into the Chapel's beautifully carved stone frames. We stood back to carefully scrutinize the windows and searched in vain as even our trained eyes could not differentiate the original glass from the replaced pieces of hand-painted glass.

At the Chapel's rededication ceremony, dignitaries and special guests assembled for the occasion. The sanctuary was animated in anticipation of the arrival of the special guest speaker. This individual had spent many Sundays of her youth here, as her father was the Pastor for the congregation at this rural English chapel. As the appointed time arrived, a warm reception was offered to the former Prime Minister of England, the honorable Margaret Thatcher.

This historic English chapel was moved from its rural setting in England to the campus of Baker University. The chancel windows above were restored by Bovard Studio and are exquisite examples of traditional English stained glass design.

Seek and ye shall find is a universal truth. The opposite of light and happiness is darkness and despair. If you were attempting to find a diamond in the earth, you would not focus your attention on the absence of diamonds. Placing your attention on the absence of something is a ridiculous way to locate it. Yet, modern psychology's technique for finding happiness is to expose the unhappiness. Placing attention on the lack of happiness can only serve to uncover more unhappiness. What we seek, we shall find. Wherever we concentrate our attention will grow and flourish. We do not remove unhappiness; we can only add happiness. When we focus our attention on happiness, happiness grows within us. This is also the nature of light and darkness. Darkness is the absence of light; we do not remove the darkness we simply add light. When entering a dark room we flick on the switch to add light. The sun rises every morning and darkness vanishes; the sun sets and darkness returns. Nevertheless, we know the sun will soon rise again and we will once again enjoy the light of day. Such is the nature of life. When we are unhappy, we should put our attention on happiness and we will find happiness. The greatest disability in life is a bad attitude. – R. B.

Rendering of a stained glass wall approximately 30 feet high by 25 feet wide (9.14m x 7.62m) for the entrance of a Baptismal chapel for a Texas church. Note the two sets of double stained glass entrance doors in the lower left and lower right.

Nativity window for the Santa Clara Mission Cemetery San Jose, California.

Resurrection window for the Santa Clara Mission Cemetery San Jose, California.

Yet the enlightened know that all manifest glories are transcended by the most humble among us, he who simply closes his eyes and becomes one with God and creation. In that absolute silence, stillness beyond imagination, at rest yet fully awake, his consciousness is bathed in the peace and bliss of the kingdom of God that lies within us all. – R. B.

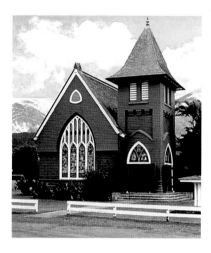

Waioli Hui'ia Church has been designated a National Historic Landmark. It is located in Hanalei, Kaua'i, Hawaii.

Figurative, abstract, traditional, minimal, modern, ornate, bright contrasting colors, or with subtle shades. Whether housed in a great cathedral or a humble country church, stained glass at its best should reflect the soul of the congregation, the spirit of God manifest on Earth. - R. B.

HURRICANE INIKI

Waioli Hui'ia Church sits at the old Mission founded in 1834 on Kauai, in the heart of Hanalei. On September 11, 1992 at 1 a.m., hurricane Iniki swept across Kauai with sustained winds of one hundred sixty miles per hour and wind gusts recorded at two hundred and twenty miles per hour. Hurricane Iniki was a big one by any standards. The Waioli Hui'ia Church was literally lifted off if its foundation, causing extensive damage to the building's structure and smashing the Church's precious stained glass heritage. The proud church had been designated a National Historic Landmark but it is much more than a landmark to the regional community of Hanalei and to all citizens of Hawaii.

The Queen of Kauai, Deborah Kapule was an early Christian convert and helped establish the Mission in the 1830's on land provided by Governor Kaikioewa of Kauai. The historic Mission House was built in 1837 and the adjoining Mission Hall was finished in 1843, resplendent with its tower belfry and requisite mission bell. The current church building was constructed on this site in 1912 and the original Mission

House and Mission Hall were fully restored that same year. The church has enjoyed an uninterrupted succession of services since 1834, first as a Congregational Church and since 1957 as a United Church of Christ.

In the aftermath of hurricane Iniki the restoration committee appointed Alfonso J. Garza, of Designare Architects in Honolulu, as the restoration architect and Callahan Construction of Hanalei, Hawaii, was awarded the general contract. They conducted a national search for a qualified stained glass studio to restore the heavily damaged windows and recreate the destroyed stained glass. Their search eventually brought them to our studio and after many discussions and consultations we were awarded the contract. It struck me that the geographic contrasts could not be greater. Bovard Studio, surrounded by the cornfields and big blue sky of Iowa, and the Waioli Hui'ia Church sitting at the base of a volcano on one of the most beautiful islands in the world. We were two disparate partners with one noble and unified objective.

In November of 1993 our restoration team arrived at the Waioli Hui'ia Church, to extract the windows. The process begins by first assessing the damage and then photographically recording the current condition of windows, it is important to have accurate site records that often prove invaluable during the restoration. The windows were carefully removed and all previously recovered bits and pieces were located before everything was crated for shipment to our studio back in Iowa.

Four sets of double lancet stained glass windows had to be recreated. Matching historic opalescent stained glass is exponentially more difficult than matching paint color or dye lots. In glass, we not only have to match a unique combination of color mix, but we must match the density and the unique refractory qualities of the light as it passes through the glass.

We put out a call to our trusted suppliers and opalescent glass manufacturers to search their hoard of old glass for suitable matches. To our delight, they successfully located a match for all the replacement glass we needed, except one. The main background glass for all of the Waioli Hui'ia Church's stained glass windows was a green, amber and white opalescent that was not currently available. We looked at dozens of color samples from current production glass and decided to ask Youghiogheny Opalescent Glass Company to recreate a glass to match the original. Their skilled colorists were able to achieve a nearly perfect match. However since the density, color and consistency of opalescent glass actually changes during the course of batch production, it was the glass three-fourths of the way through the batch that was selected as the best match.

The restored windows were shipped 4,000 miles back to Kauai and meticulously reinstalled into the rebuilt Waioli Hui'ai Church in time for the Church's dedication ceremonies in April of 1994. We were thrilled with the results as was the restoration architect and the church's congregation. We have been told that even the most discerning visitor is amazed to learn the stained glass windows have undergone extensive restoration.

15

CLEANING AND MAINTENANCE OF LEADED GLASS WINDOWS

The good news is stained glass windows do not show dirt and grime as readily as a clear glass window does. However, there is a course of action that you can take to keep your new windows looking immaculate or to bring back the luster to an older installation.

The primary cleaning for a stained glass window is to simply dust the inside surface occasionally with a soft brush. When a more meticulous cleaning is required, it is important to be conscientious of any painted areas on the window. Painted stained glass and particularly areas with enamel paint (opaque colors) are especially sensitive to acids, which means a vinegar and water solution could easily damage these areas. Be sure to test all painted areas with your cleaning solution prior to any thorough cleaning and avoid any areas in doubt. If your testing finds the painted areas to be stable, they may be safely cleaned along with the non-painted areas of the window.

Stained glass windows should be washed using a soft cotton cloth and a pH neutral cleaning solution mixed with distilled water.

Detail St. Cecilia window.

St. Cecilia window for the St. Cecilia Church in Ames, Iowa.

When cleaning a stained glass window, such as this panel depicting "The Ascension of Christ", it is important to be conscientious of the painted areas as they are especially sensitive to cleaning solutions containing acids, including vinegar and water. Be sure to test all painted areas on either new or historic stained glass windows with your cleaning solution prior to any thorough cleaning and avoid any areas in doubt. If your testing finds the painted areas to be stable, they may be safely cleaned along with the non-painted areas of the window.

Stained glass windows should be washed using a soft cotton cloth and a pH neutral cleaning solution mixed with distilled water. An excellent product is Triton X-100, a professional quality, non-ionic detergent (made by City Chemical Company of NY). However, most horse shampoos (available from any equine tack shop) are a safe and very effective alternative for cleaning stained glass windows. Since horse skin is more sensitive than human skin, horse shampoos are formulated to be pH neutral. Some cleaning compounds to be avoided are any that contain acids (such as vinegar), ammonia, and/or abrasives and never use scouring powders or steel wool scrubbers.

If your test cleaning indicates that the painted areas are unstable, especially if you found loose or flaking areas, it is better to leave the dirt on the stained glass rather than chance further damage to the window. Unstable paint could be the consequence of age, or may indicate the original artist used an improper paint formula or incorrect kiln firing procedure. Some historic stained glass windows were actually "cold painted" using standard air-dry paints that can easily be scraped or washed off the glass. When the window reaches the point of requiring a complete restoration, a qualified stained glass restoration company will address the problem of the unstable glass paint.

Installation of a restored Tiffany window including exterior laminated glass protective covering.

In addition to an occasional cleaning, the steel reinforcing system needs to be checked periodically to ensure it remains attached to the window's lead matrix. As leaded glass windows age, normal expansion and contraction may break the copper tie wires away from the round steel reinforcing bars. Or, if the more modern flat steel reinforcing bars are used, the solder joints connecting them to the lead matrix of your stained glass windows can break loose. The reinforcing bars need to be reattached to the lead matrix by repairing the wires or solder joints. This is a job for a professional stained glass restoration company. Windows assembled with dividing steel T-bars need to be inspected periodically for rust on the steel. If found the corrosion must be removed and the surface repainted.

Finally, windows set into their frames with glaziers putty should have any loose or missing putty replaced on a regular basis. To maintain a strong physical integrity, a stained glass window depends on a solid setting and tight installation.

Time and money spent on preventative maintenance will save money in the end as it prolongs the life of your stained glass and delays the time until costly restoration will be required. Few products made today are expected to last for centuries. Stained glass windows have a long life expectancy and a good maintenance program will preserve your stained glass heritage for centuries.

Above and Right: This series of four historic windows were originally created by the famous stained glass artist Frederick Lamb. They were releaded and restored by Bovard Studio for The First Presbyterian Church, Davenport, Iowa.

Above & Right: New installation of a series of stained glass windows for a chapel at The First United Methodist Church, Fairfield, Iowa.

New stained glass windows for The First United Methodist Church, Fairfield, Iowa.

FACETED GLASS (DALLE DE VERRE) WINDOWS

FACETED GLASS WINDOWS

Dalle de verre (French for "tiles of glass") also called faceted glass windows, use one inch (2.5 cm) thick slabs of glass, cut into the desired shapes then selectively faceted on the interior edges to enhance the refraction of light. The design process for a dalle de verre window is similar to that of a leaded glass window. However, the fabrication process is entirely different. The cut and faceted pieces of glass are arranged on a casting table according to the pattern design. Then an epoxy resin is poured between each piece to create the structural matrix. Finally, the resin is covered with a layer of colored granules. We strongly recommend the use of black or very dark colored granules unless a very specific effect is desired. The black colored matrix will result in a uniform presentation on the exterior of the building, much like a solid sheet of glass. A light colored matrix seems to produce an unsettling disorder that often conflicts with the architecture of the building.

Above: Dalle de verre or faceted glass windows are fabricated using one inch (2.5 cm) thick slabs of glass. An epoxy resin is poured between each glass piece to create the structural matrix, which shows as black lines in the photograph.

Faceted glass window, for Branson Hills Assembly of God, Branson, Missouri.

While a protective covering is not required for faceted glass, many architects specify a bronze or tinted sheet of exterior glazing to minimize the impact of the faceted window's resin matrix on the design of their building. In faceted glass windows, the negative space (the matrix) is even more notable than in the design of a leaded glass window, and its impact on the finished artwork is much more pronounced.

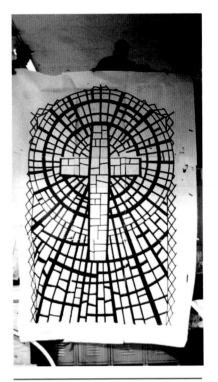

Above: Full scale layout pattern for a faceted glass window; the area that will be filled with epoxy are indicated with heavy black lines.

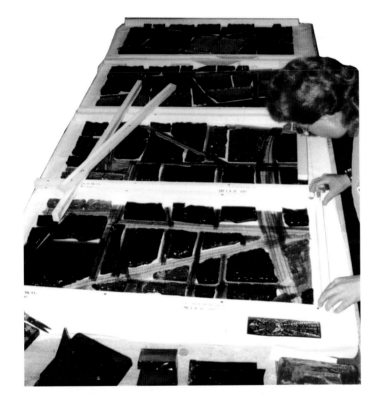

Above left: Faceted glass fabricator Brian Sullender, lays the dalle's and positions the edge blocks prior to "investing" or pouring the epoxy compound between the glass pieces.

Proposal rendering for a series of faceted glass panels with minimal emblematic representation.

Faceted Glass

CARE AND MAINTENANCE OF FACETED GLASS WINDOWS

Properly formulated and fabricated faceted glass windows, made with an epoxy matrix, should require no maintenance other than repairing loose glaziers putty or construction sealant around the perimeter of the panels where they are set into the frame.

However, older faceted glass windows fabricated with a portland cement matrix may require extensive repairs and restoration over time. A professional stained glass restoration company should be consulted for problems on this type of window.

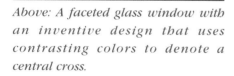

Above: A faceted glass window with an inventive design that uses contrasting colors to denote a central cross.

Right: A Computer aided rendition for a faceted glass window with a contemporary design. Notice the creative use of rectangles as a background grid.

Right two photos: A Faceted glass rose window depicting Luther's Seal for St. Peter's Church Schaumburg, Illinois. Exterior view of the window during installation, it is illuminated from inside the building with supplementary lighting.

Below: Faceted glass windows designed for St. Peter's. Church Schaumburg, Illinois. This design set consisted of 12 windows featuring the life of Christ.

ᎪMID THE HILLS of north central Alabama, shrouded in early morning fog set ablaze by the afternoon sun, you will find the unassuming seat of the reign of silence. A profound spiritual silence, produced by the purity of monastic lives, enables a common civilian such as myself to feel God's presence.

Dedications abound with "God incarnate" and "Christ the King", His name and form shapes this holy atmosphere in addition to the ceaseless devotion of a small brotherhood of traditional Benedictine Monks devoted to the ancient ways of the Roman Catholic Church.

Father Leonard, devoted priest, faithfully followed a steady course along the straight and narrow path of life-long dedication to his Church. Then soon after the implementation of Vatican II, he found himself at large in the wilderness outside of mother Church. His life of single-minded devotion to God soon energized the forces of nature to reward Father Leonard's purity of heart. A parcel of property was secured and a small group of devoted like-minded souls united to raise Christ the King Abbey surrounded by the ancient forest in the hills of Alabama.

On my most recent trip to the Abbey, I was accompanied by my three youngest sons, Michael 15, Matthew 13, and 8 year old Johnny. As we wound our way up the serpentine driveway in our pickup truck, complete with camper and speedboat, these robust and dynamic boys quickly zeroed in on the Abbey as a spiritual beacon. Our motley crew became uncharacteristically tranquil as we approached the refuge. Cramped from long days of driving, my boys stumbled out of our cluttered truck inspired and awe-struck by the serene and holy atmosphere. We were warmly greeted by Father Abbot and the Monks who reverently showed my sons the monastery church, which was built using very sketchy plans combined with much prayer and manual labor.

New installation of stained glass for Christ the King Abbey, Cullman, Alabama.

Interior view of Christ the King Abbey, note the circular window above the alter.

Now nearly complete, the Abbey is a repository of ancient knowledge and holy artifacts, which includes one of the most precious of all holy relics, a splinter from the cross upon which Christ was crucified. My sons, now completely taken up with the sacred ambience, were shown the historic personification of the saints as illustrated in the Gothic style stained glass windows that were created by our studio for the Abbey.

Soon enough my sons discovered Ginger, a stray dog adopted by the Abbey and while they all enjoyed a romp in the sun, the Monks and I discussed the design and plans for the monastery's final stained glass window, "Christ the King" (see this window on page 107).

Nearing the end of our day, we were led down to the cool chambers of the guest dining room located under the sanctuary. Once there, we were treated to a vegetarian feast. As we quietly dined, we were enthralled by the echoes of the Monk's Gregorian chants of holy praise drifting down the corridors as they dined separately from us in ancient monastic tradition.

For the remainder of the trip, no matter how fine the restaurant, my sons would often remark, "Dad this food is good, but not as good as the food at the monastery!"

New installation of stained glass for Christ the King Abbey, Cullman, Alabama.

Exterior view of St. Martin Church, Tower, Minnesota. The stained glass windows are to be installed in the openings seen here in the rotunda sanctuary.

LORD OF CREATION

This project for St. Martin Church depicts the changing of the seasons. The building project specified windows that would have the top half blocked from view due to the way the window's installation creates indirect lighting for the worship space. Our proposal offered a creative solution for this special requirement.

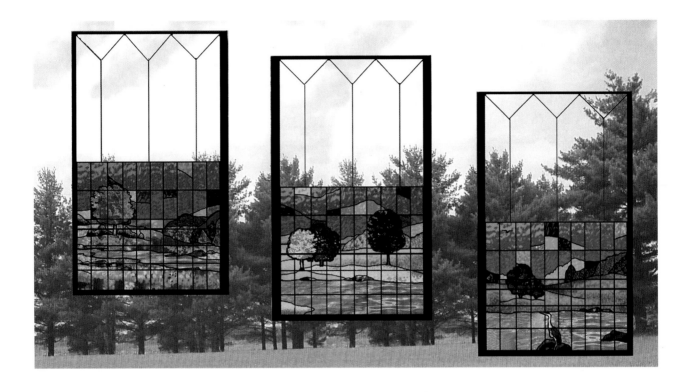

St. Martin Church, Tower, Minnesota

A proposal for a new faceted glass installation for *Victorious Believers Church, Saginaw, Michigan.* The central section (the warm color section) is set back approximately 6' (1.8m) from the front surface. This creates an entrance and exit passageway in the chancel area for service leaders and other participants.

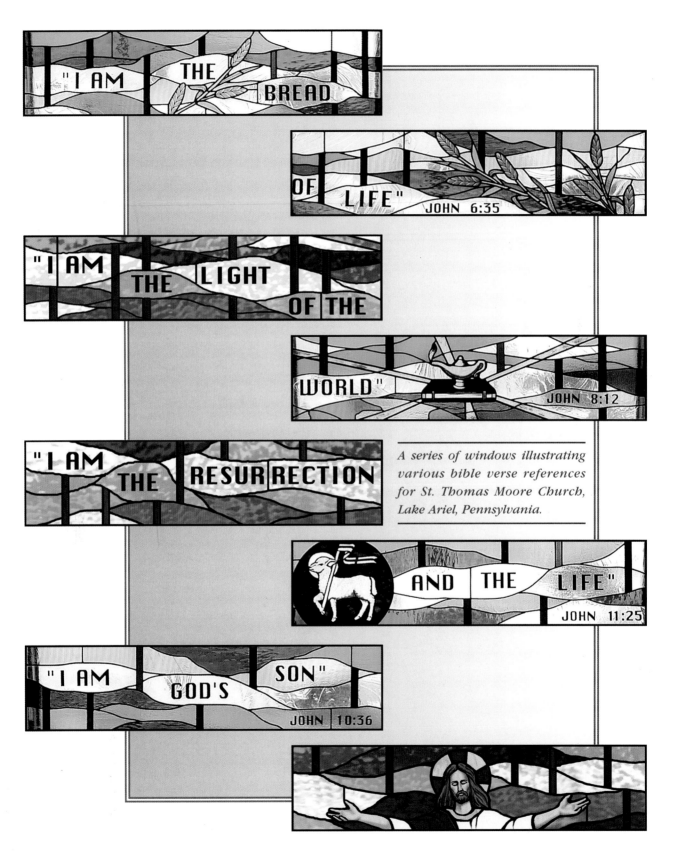

"I AM THE BREAD OF LIFE" JOHN 6:35

"I AM THE LIGHT OF THE WORLD" JOHN 8:12

"I AM THE RESURRECTION AND THE LIFE" JOHN 11:25

"I AM GOD'S SON" JOHN 10:36

A series of windows illustrating various bible verse references for St. Thomas Moore Church, Lake Ariel, Pennsylvania.

MASONIC RETIREMENT CENTER, ARLINGTON, TEXAS

The long curving "Dallas style" driveway and extended horizontal lines of the Masonic home for aged Masons, called to mind of the significant history of this organization. Masonic Orders revolutionized feudal Europe with their spiritual and philosophical teachings which advanced the freeing of the serfs and led to the beginning of democratic government, culminating in a substantial contribution to the founding principles of the United States of America.

George Washington was the commander of his Masonic lodge and most of the signers of the Declaration of Independence were Freemasons. Our great nation was founded upon many principles of Freemasonry.

We were delighted to receive the contract to design and build the stained glass windows for the Masonic home's chapel. We worked closely with the Masons working out the computer aided designs for the renderings, communicating back and forth both graphically and verbally to get the designs and coloring of their symbolism exactly right for their chapel stained glass windows.

George Washington was the commander of his Masonic lodge and most of the signers of the Declaration of Independence were members of the Freemasons. For this reason alone it could be said that the Masonic philosophy contributed to the founding principles of the United States of America.

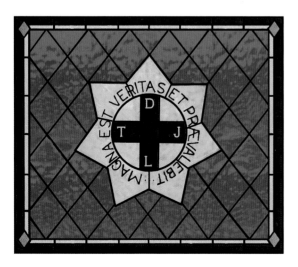

This series of new windows were designed for The Masonic Retirement Center Chapel in Arlington, Texas. The colors and attributes of this organization's distinctive symbolism has considerable significance and had to be exactly right for their chapel windows.

THE MYSTERIOUS EAST with its more than 5,000 year old Vedic culture has much to offer the West. Many of their age-old herbal formulas have been proven to have dramatic effects on improving health without the side effects of our western pharmaceuticals. Eastern spiritual practices and philosophies are having an increasing impact on our own culture and world view. The recent revival of ancient meditation techniques is gaining popularity in the West. Significant bodies of scientific research are proving profound health benefits from these ancient practices and herbal formulas. That may help account for the practitioners' empirical reports of finding inner peace and fulfillment.

We are fortunate on occasion to be commissioned to create stained glass windows for this time-honored traditional culture. There is no better way to express the religious heritage and culture of ancient India, whose goal is enlightenment, than through the medium of light. As suriya, the sun moves across the eternal sky, each day new light is transformed by the stained glass window into art radiating through the inner space of the installations environment into the viewers eyes, mind, and soul.

Hanuman has a powerful, muscular body and the superior intellect of a yogi. As the quintessential devotee he represents physical prowess, mental discipline and spiritual purity.

Lakshmi represents wealth, fortune, power, beauty, and abundance. She is enchantingly beautiful draped in a red sari, standing on a lotus blossom and holding lotus flowers in her hands. The white elephant, symbol of rain clouds showers her with water to bring life to parched land.

Ganesha or Ganapati is the destroyer of all obstacles. He also represents education, knowledge, wisdom, literature, and the fine arts. This window was designed and built for a restaurant in Davenport, Iowa.

A TIFFANY WINDOW RESTORATION

RESTORING AN ORIGINAL TIFFANY WINDOW

The restoration of any historic window is a great responsibility for both the window's trustee and the contractor. The owner or trustee of the stained glass window must ensure that the restoration company has the training and experience to undertake all necessary work in a professional manner. References should be provided (and checked) and an extensive plan of action must be submitted by the contractor outlining the full extent of restoration, including adherence to historic conservation procedures. Comprehensive insurance must be engaged to safeguard against any perils that could occur to the window during removal, rebuilding and re-installation or at the very least the building's current insurance coverage needs to be extended for off premises work.

Right: An Exquisite window by L. C. Tiffany & Co. installed in St. Lukes United Methodist Church in Dubuque, Iowa, restored by Bovard Studio.

When prestigious works by distinguished artists such as a L.C. Tiffany, J. LaFarge, F.L. Wright, or others needs to be restored, it may be advisable to engage the services of a professional conservation consultant, specializing in stained glass restoration. They will advise the trustee on the extent of work necessary and inform them on specific technical requirements to ensure that irreversible restoration methods are not undertaken. Historic restoration is definitely a job that is worth doing right and should be entrusted only to those who have proven to be trustworthy.

The first step in restoring any historic stained glass window is to document its current physical state and appearance. It is of the utmost importance to photograph the stained glass window in both transmitted and reflected light prior to removing it from its frame.

Take several photos of the window with transmitted light, (natural light passing through the stained glass) without flash and being careful that the interior lighting is extinguished. Since the exposure time will be longer (due to lower available light) it is advisable to mount the camera on a tripod when taking photographs from the interior side of the stained glass window.

The first step in restoring any historic stained glass window is to document its current physical state and appearance.

Here Tess Bovard and Carrie Thomas take photographs of each stained glass panel (or section) of the windows in the restoration project. Detailed photographs are taken of specific areas with extensive damage such as cracked glass, missing areas of glass, badly damaged paint, etc.

Above: Paul Conly of Bovard Studio preparing to remove a section of Tiffany's "Job" window.

Tiffany Restoration

Above: Here we see the panels placed into a wooden packing crate with foam rubber sheeting to separate and protect the fragile panels during transport.

Next make a record of the interior and exterior surfaces of the stained glass window in reflected light (lighted from the same side as the camera). The sun's light will usually suffice for the exterior photos but a supplemental flash may be needed for the interior surface photographs. Separate photos should be taken for each stained glass panel (section) of the window, plus detailed photos of specific areas with extensive damage such as cracked glass, missing areas of glass, badly damaged paint, etc. Additional photographic documentation may be made back at the studio if required.

Prepare the windows for removal by securing loose and/or broken pieces of glass with conservators tape. It is always advisable to secure the entire width and length of the panel with tape, especially if the window's structure is weak and fragile. It is important to check any painted areas for stability prior to placing conservators tape on these surfaces. If the glass paint is unstable or the stability of the paint is in doubt, the painted side of the stained glass must not be taped. Once the panels have been secured, they are carefully removed from the window frame and placed into wooden packing crates with foam rubber sheeting to separate and protect the fragile panels during transport. We pickup and deliver the panels in our own trucks.

Right: Mickey Bar and Paul Conly of Bovard Studio are shown here carrying a section of Tiffany's "Job" window. Note the conservators tape placed on the panel to enhance stability during shipping.

Once back at the shop, the extracted stained glass windows are prepared for restoration. The first panel is placed onto the glazing bench where more notes are taken and more photographs made (if necessary). Then a rubbing is made for each section of the window by placing vellum paper over the window and rubbing colored oil pastels (or artists charcoal) over the lead lines to create a full size pattern of the lead matrix. This pattern will be used later for reassembly. If the section contains plating, as the Tiffany window in the illustration does, a separate rubbing is made for each layer of plate. These additional plate rubbings are done on top of the first rubbing using a different colored pastel for each successive layer of plating (a rubbing is made after each plate layer is removed). This will show the fabricator how each plate is "registered" on the window during reassembly. Notes are taken of the size, profile and description of each lead came or copper foil area within the stained glass window and this is recorded directly on the rubbing. Then two copies of each rubbing are made one for reference and one as a working copy.

The restoration specialist must be sure that sufficient records have been made to ensure an exact reconstruction can be achieved. Only then are the stained glass panels carefully disassembled. The lead came is cut away and one glass piece at a time is removed and placed in it's correct location on the working copy of the rubbing. During disassembly it is important to keep a sample of each different lead came size and profile or a section of the copperfoil assembly for reference and documentation.

A close-up side view of a Tiffany window showing the use of molded glass for the flower. Note how the flower petals protrude from the surface of the window.

Above & Right: Detail photograph of the same figure shown before and after cleaning and restoration. The difference is dramatic especially in the angel's hair and wings.

The lead came is cut away and one glass piece at a time is removed and placed in it's correct location on the working copy of the rubbing. During disassembly it is important to keep a sample of each different lead came size and profile or a section of the copperfoil assembly for reference and documentation. The window shown above is a section from the stained glass ceiling in the Montana State Capital, Senate Chamber.

When the entire panel has been disassembled it must be cleaned and inspected. Each piece of non-painted glass is cleaned with Triton X-100, a professional quality, non-ionic detergent (made by City Chemical Company of NY) or an equivalent pH neutral glass cleaner mixed with distilled water. Prior to cleaning, painted areas of the window must be tested to determine that the paint is stable. If it is, these areas should be gently cleaned with a soft cotton cloth and distilled water. Unstable painted areas need be stabilized. The basic treatment is to coat the painted surface with a clear sealant to bond the remaining paint to the glass. However, it is intensely important that the sealant used be chemically compatible with the underlying paint to ensure no further damage is induced. For this reason it is necessary to consult an expert restoration specialist to determine the appropriate consolidation method for the particular problem encountered. Areas where the paint is badly faded, has been washed away, or otherwise lost, should be restored by first treating the existing paint with the clear sealant. Then the missing details are painted onto a new piece of 1/16" (1.5 mm) or thinner clear glass that is plated over the original painted stained glass. This ensures the historic work remains unaltered and undisturbed and makes the restoration fully reversible in the future.

Above: Face of an Angel from Tiffany window. Image on left is the top plate showing detailed glass painting. The image on right has painted highlights and is one level of three base plates in this plated section (see page 45 lower right photo).

Above: Interior of St. Luke United Methodist Church showing the restored "Job" window (on right) among the other exquisite Tiffany Windows.

Cracked and broken pieces of stained glass are repaired by edge gluing with clear Hxtel™ epoxy (a commercial brand product), clear silicone, or by copper foiling and soldering the pieces together. The specific repair method will be decided based upon what is best for the historic preservation of the particular stained glass window.

Missing pieces of art glass can sometimes be closely matched from the more than 4,000 colors, densities and textures that are manufactured and available today. Sometimes two pieces of glass are plated or overlaid to achieve the best possible match. In some cases where a glass making formula is known, a glass manufacturer may be willing to custom create a particular stained glass sheet to match a destroyed original piece. This is an expensive alternative but if the missing glass is dominant in the design or if the window is an exceptional work, this may be the best solution.

The various sizes and profiles of lead came also need to be closely matched. Many of the came profiles are available as standard stock items manufactured from existing dies, however other more specialized shapes may need to be specially ordered from custom or rarely used dies and depending on the importance of the window, may be a necessary step.

Once all the glass has been cleaned, broken pieces repaired, missing pieces replaced, painted pieces replicated, and all other materials are obtained, the stained glass window is ready to be reassembled. The pieces will be placed on the working copy of the rubbing, precisely as the window was originally created. The fabrication will be carried out by skilled craftsmen in essentially the same tried and true method as the window was fabricated decades before.

Above: We can can usually closely match the missing pieces from the more than 4000 art glass selections manufactured and available today.

Left: The fabrication will be carried out by skilled craftsmen in essentially the same tried and true method as it was decades before. This plated window is a restoration for First Evangelical Lutheran Church, Altoona PA.

Above: Detail of Tiffany window at St.Lukes United Methodist Church, Dubuque, Iowa.

The Tiffany window we are restoring here has complex plated sections that will require the fabricator to devise an assembly of lead cames to create a shape otherwise not available. They will solder several strips and/or layers of came together to create a shape based on the sample saved during disassembly. We have found that a modern improvement can be made to the original structure of plated sections by applying a silicone seal around the edges of the stacked plates of glass. This will prevent dirt and water from collecting between the plates, which cannot be cleaned without disassembling the window. Contamination of plated sections is a major problem encountered in historic windows that include extensive plating.

Any structural deficiencies in the original windows should be addressed to prevent the premature failure of the window in the future. One major structural remedy is to use lead came that has sufficient tensile strength. It is crucial to use a lead came manufactured by the extrusion process using a lead alloy that contains antimony, silver, copper, or tin. The original stained glass window was probably fabricated using pure milled lead (without alloy additives) which is comparatively soft and malleable (lead alloy came is a recent development). This improvement alone will greatly increase the expected longevity of the stained glass restoration. Another common structural deficiency is the use of a single layer of relatively thin glass, usually 1/8" (3 mm), in the borders. This fragile border is required to support the heavy weight of the central glass section and is particularly troublesome in windows with multiple plates of glass which add

Left: Preparing the pieces for reassembly. Notice the book in upper left corner with photos and notes about the original window. Here the fabricator is applying a silicone seal around the edges of the stacked plated sections of glass. This will prevent dirt and water from collecting between the plates after installation.

considerable weight. Unfortunately, this situation often results in the folding and sometimes total collapse of the border, especially at the base and lower sides of the window. A simple, reversible, non-invasive remedy for this deficiency is to apply a second plate of clear glass to the border areas on the exterior side of the window, thereby doubling the strength of the borders.

When fabrication is complete, the window must be cemented with a glazing cement specifically formulated for leaded windows. The cementing process packs the space between the flanges of the lead came and the stained glass with a sealant to stiffen and strengthen the window as well as weatherproof it. Most cement compounds have a black dye component to enhance the surface the new "silvery colored" lead with a dark, richly colored patina to give it a more mature appearance.

During a restoration such as this Tiffany window, we take special notice of areas with the most structural damage. These areas of distress

Hand packing the Flanges of the came with glazing putty for a panel of the Tiffany "Job" window from St. Luke United Methodist Church in Dubuque, Iowa.

Detail of the Tiffany window showing before and after cleaning and restoration. Turn to page 89 for a close-up side view of this window to see how the flower is a 3-dimensional molded component.

Above: One of the most effective structural engineering solutions is to attach brass rebar directly to the lead. Notice the placement of horizontal bars in the above window.

may be due to an insufficient supporting structure or to weaknesses within the windows design. Whatever the reason it is our responsibility to correct the problem in the least intrusive way. Obviously these areas require additional structural engineering and one of the most effective solutions is to attach brass rebar directly to the lead in the structurally deficient areas of the window. This rebar is a flat brass rod, 1/16" (1.5 mm) thick and anywhere from 1/4" to 1" (6.3 to 25.4 mm) wide. It is soldered directly to the lead came, perpendicular (90°) to the face, on the exterior side of the window. Preferably these rebars should be kept as straight as possible but they may be bent to follow along the length of a gently curving lead line. This technique structurally reinforces the stained glass window with minimum aesthetic impact (see example of this on page 59, at top right).

While the stained glass window is "in the shop" undergoing restoration, it's an opportune time to take up the necessary repairs and restoration to the window's frame. In some extreme cases the frame may need to be totally replaced, at the very least it should be cleaned, sealed and refinished. If the window restoration company does not provide these services, a qualified carpenter should be called to make an assessment of the frame's integrity and complete the repairs.

The culmination of any restoration is the reinstallation. Above: the restored Tiffany window is returned to its rightful home.

The culmination of any restoration is the time of reinstallation, when the restored window is returned to its rightful home. A scrupulously restored window, with structural weaknesses remedied and installed with a properly vented protective covering (see page 54-55), can be expected to last significantly longer than the original stained glass window, before it will require another restoration.

It is a very gratifying experience to return a Tiffany or other historic stained glass window to its original appearance and condition. It is rewarding to witness the dramatic contrast between the dirty, deteriorated, misshapen window of the past to the richness of color and structural integrity of the restored installation. It is a thrill to return the many lost details of a window, details that seemed to be hidden in the past and are now mysteriously resurrected into the living present.

Above: Paul Conly (left) and Mike Swope (right) install one section the restored Tiffany window.

Below: The completed and installed restoration of the Tiffany "Job" window for St. Lukes United Methodist Church Dubuque, Iowa.

THE DESIGN ARCHIVE

The designs on the following 60 pages presents a cross section of work taken from Bovard Studio's portfolio. From simple to complex, from abstract to representational, from traditional to modern, and from small intimate stained glass windows to windows as big as the side of a building. The techniques used to fabricate these windows vary from leaded glass to faceted glass. Some have no glass painting, others have every piece of glass in the window painted. Some windows have etching, others have silver staining, plating, traditional glass staining colors, transparent and opaque enamels, stenciling, silk screening and/or medallions. Most windows have a combination of several of these treatments

On these pages you will find a wide variety of what is possible in ecclesiastic art glass today. It is my hope that you will find inspiration from a few of them, and it will be a step in your continued exploration of the art and the craft of stained glass.

BAPTISM
Leaded, unpainted
Rectangle
Reference B11

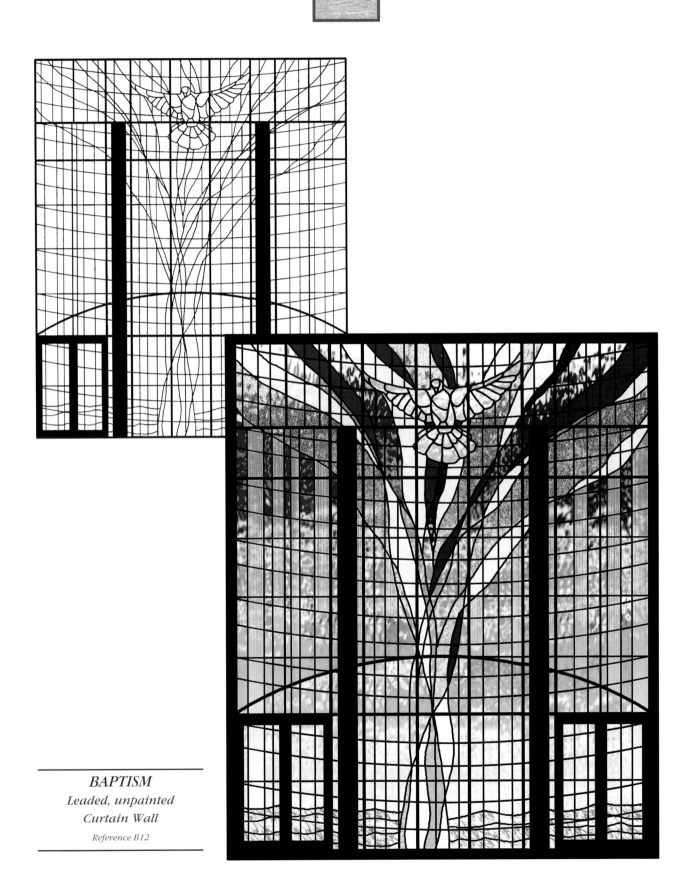

BAPTISM
Leaded, unpainted
Curtain Wall

Reference B12

YESTERDAY, TODAY, FOREVER
Graphical Logo
Round
Reference B13

HOLY SPIRIT

Transitional

Round

Reference B14

BRIDAL DOME
Victorian
Ceiling Dome

Reference B15

OUR MISSION
Traditional
Round

Reference B16

HOLY SPIRIT
Transitional
Round

Reference B14

BRIDAL DOME
Victorian
Ceiling Dome

Reference B15

OUR MISSION
Traditional
Round

Reference B16

ROSE WINDOW
Traditional
Round

Reference B17

LUTHER'S SEAL
Traditional
Round

Reference B18

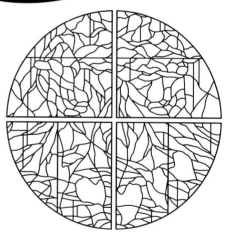

COME UNTO ME
Modern, some painting
Round

Reference B19

HOLY SPIRIT
Traditional
Round

Reference B20

LAST SUPPER
Figurative, traditional
Round

Reference B21

GOOD SHEPHERD
BLESSING THE CHILDREN
Figurative, full painted
Round

Reference B22

SAINT GREGORY THE GREAT
Gothic, figurative, painted
Top Round Classic

Reference B23

SAINT BONIFACE
Gothic, figurative, painted
Top Round Classic

Reference B24

CHRIST THE KING
Gothic, figurative, painted
Top Round Classic

Reference B25

ANGEL
Traditional, figurative, painted
Rectangle
Reference B27

ANGEL
Traditional, figurative, painted
Rectangle
Reference B26

FIVE MARTYRED NUNS
Modern, figurative
Top Round, rectangle

Reference B29

CHRIST THE GOOD SHEPHERD
Transitional, figurative
Top round, rectangle

Reference B28

ANGEL
Figurative, painted
Gothic, modified trefoil
Reference B30

CHRIST THE KING
Figurative, painted
Triptych
Reference B31

MADONNA WITH ANGELS
Figurative, painted
Gothic triptych

Reference B32

CHRIST PRAYING IN THE GARDEN OF GETHSEMANE
Figurative, painted
Gothic, double lancet
Reference B33

CHRIST AT THE DOOR
Figurative, painted
Rectangle

Reference B34

LILIES
Traditional
Rectangle

Reference B35

BEHEADING OF JOHN
Figurative, painted
Top round rectangle

Reference B36

BAPTISM OF CHRIST
Standard figurative
Rectangle
Reference B37

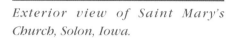

Exterior view of Saint Mary's Church, Solon, Iowa.

Interior view of half diamond window installation

SAINT MARY

Transitional Figurative
Half diamond, triangle

Reference B38

SAINT RITA
Transitional Figurative
Half diamond, triangle

Reference B39

COME UNTO ME
Modern figurative
Rectangle
Reference B40

TEMPTATION OF CHRIST
Modern figurative
Rectangle
Reference B41

THE NETS ARE OVERFLOWING
*Modern figurative
Rectangle*

Reference B42

LAST SUPPER
*Modern figurative
Rectangle*

Reference B43

ANNUNCIATION
*Modern figurative
Rectangle*

Reference B44

JESUS CALMS
THE STORM
Modern figurative
Rectangle
Reference B45

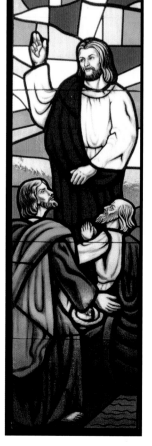

CHRIST TEACHING
THE DISCIPLES
Modern figurative
Rectangle
Reference B46

THE RISEN CHRIST
APPEARS TO MARY
Modern figurative
Rectangle
Reference B47

LAZARUS IS RAISED FROM THE DEAD
Modern figurative
Rectangle

Reference B48

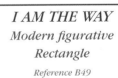

I AM THE WAY
Modern figurative
Rectangle

Reference B49

NATIVITY
Modern figurative
Rectangle

Reference B50

THE LAST SUPPER
Modern figurative
Rectangle
Reference B51

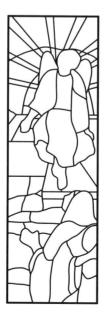

THE EMPTY TOMB
Modern figurative
Rectangle
Reference B52

The Good Shepherd
Figurative, simple
Primitive arch

Reference B54

THE GARDEN OF GETHSEMANE
Grisaille background
Gothic arch

Reference B53

The Good Shepherd
Figurative, traditional
Rectangle

Reference B55

CHRIST WALKS ON THE WATER
Transitional, figurative
Rectangle
Reference B56

SUFFER THE LITTLE CHILDREN TO COME UNTO ME
Figurative, grisaille background
Modified top round
Reference B57

GETHSEMANE
Figurative, grisaille background
Modified top round
Reference B58

CRUCIFIXION
Figurative, standard
Rectangle

Reference B59

ANNUNCIATION
Figurative, standard
Top round, rectangle

Reference B60

I GO TO PREPARE A PLACE FOR YOU
Figurative, standard
Rectangle

Reference B61

CHILD FISHING
Modern, with plating
Rectangle
Reference B62

Dogwood
Modern, with plating
Rectangle

Reference B64

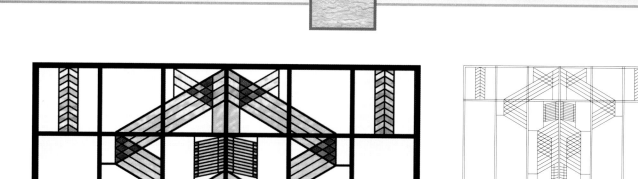

THUNDERBIRD
Prairie style
Rectangle
Reference B65

Right: Entrance lobby of the Council Bluffs Public Library, Council Bluffs, Iowa.

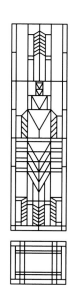

CYBORG FIGURE
Prairie style
Rectangle
Reference B67

WHEAT
Prairie style
Rectangle
Reference B66

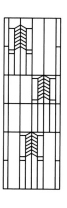

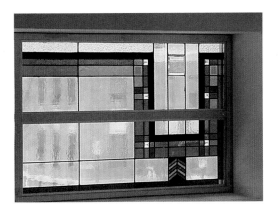

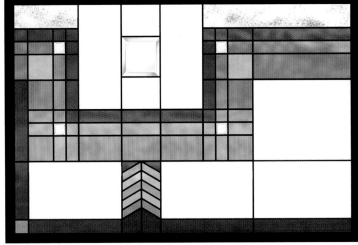

WHEAT
Prairie style
Rectangle
Reference B68

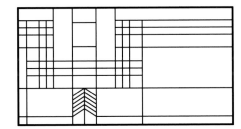

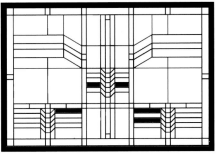

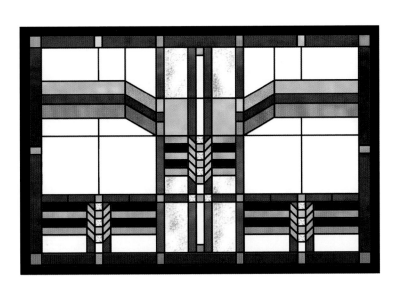

WHEAT
Prairie style
Rectangle
Reference B69

SAINT PAUL ON THE ROAD TO DAMASCUS
Figurative
Rectangle

Reference B70

ON THE ROAD TO DAMASCUS, ACTS 9:3-5A
"I am Jesus whom thou persecutest"

CHRIST THE LAMB OF GOD
Traditional
Rectangle
Reference B71

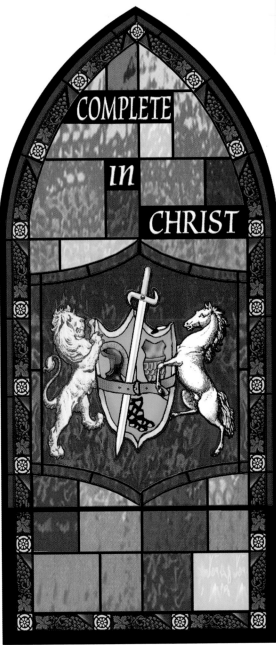

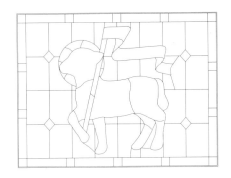

COMPLETE IN CHRIST
Traditional
Gothic arch
Reference B72

GETHSEMANE
Medallion, traditional
Rectangle

Reference B74

ROSE
Medallion, traditional
Rectangle

Reference B73

MADONNA
Medallion, traditional
Rectangle

Reference B75

CHRIST THE KING
Traditional
Modified half round

Reference B76

HOLY SPIRIT
Medallion, traditional
Gothic arch

Reference B77

I AM THE BREAD OF LIFE
Traditional
Rectangle
Reference B78

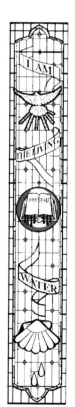

I AM THE LIVING WATER
Traditional
Rectangle
Reference B79

MARY AT THE TOMB
Contemporary, figurative
Gothic arch
Reference B81

CHRIST, COME UNTO ME
Contemporary, figurative
Gothic arch
Reference B80

COMMUNION
Contemporary
Top round, diptych

Reference B82

CHRIST IS RISEN
Contemporary
Primitive arch

Reference B83

I HAVE COME TO
SAVE THE WORLD
Contemporary
Rectangle

Reference B84

MADONNA & CHILD
Contemporary
Rectangle

Reference B85

COME UNTO ME
Contemporary
Rectangle

Reference B86

HOLY SPIRIT
Contemporary
Gothic arch
Reference B87

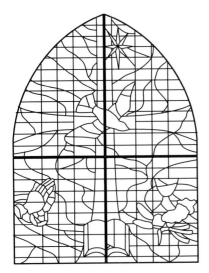

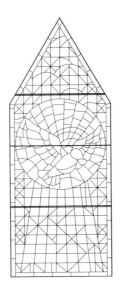

HOLY SPIRIT
Contemporary
Primitive arch
Reference B88

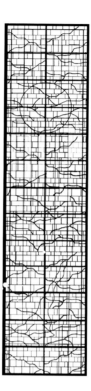

I AM THE LIGHT #1
Contemporary
Rectangle
Reference B89

I AM THE LIGHT #2
Contemporary
Rectangle
Reference B90

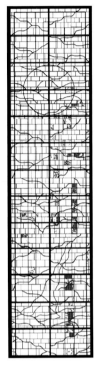

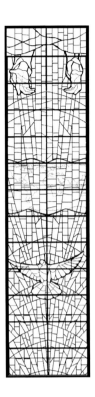

I AM THE LIGHT #3
Contemporary
Rectangle

Reference B91

PENTECOST
Contemporary
Rectangle

Reference B92

GUARDIAN ANGEL
Traditional, figurative
Triptych

Reference B93

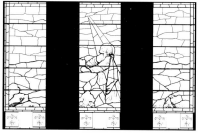

GETHSEMANE
Traditional, figurative
Triptych

Reference B94

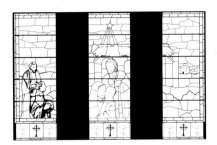

NATIVITY
Traditional, figurative
Triptych
Reference B95

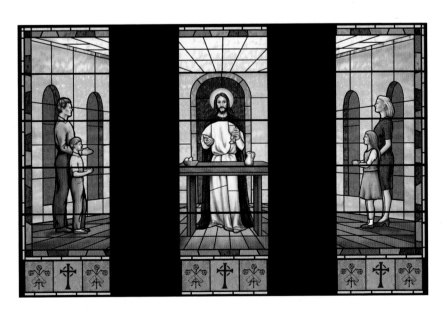

THE LAST SUPPER
Modern, figurative
Triptych
Reference B96

WOMAN AT THE WELL
Traditional, figurative
Triptych
Reference B97

ASCENSION
Traditional, figurative
Triptych
Reference B98

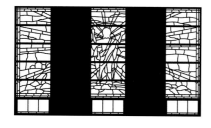

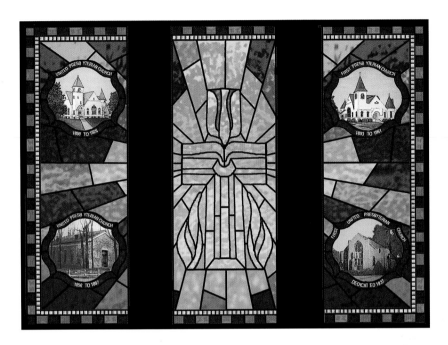

HISTORY OF OUR CHURCH
Traditional, medallion Triptych

Reference B99

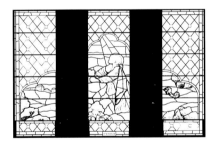

GETHSEMANE
Traditional, figurative Triptych

Reference B100

THE 14 STATIONS OF THE CROSS
Transitional, figurative
Rectangle

Reference B101

THE CROSS
Contemporary, faceted glass
Gothic arch

Reference B103

LUTHER'S SEAL
Contemporary, faceted glass
Round, rose window

Reference B104

Opposite Page:
CRUCIFIXION
Mixed media, hand-painted
traditional stained glass with a
faceted glass background
Rectangle

Reference B102

ASCENSION OF CHRIST
Contemporary, faceted
Primitive arch

Reference B105

COME UNTO ME
Contemporary, faceted
Top round, rectangle

Reference B106

SAINT CLEMENT
Contemporary, faceted
Rectangle

Reference B107

FEEDING THE MULTITUDES
Contemporary, faceted glass
Rectangle

Reference B108

TEACHING THE DISCIPLES
Contemporary, faceted glass
Rectangle

Reference B109

BAPTISM OF CHRIST
Contemporary, faceted glass
Rectangle

Reference B110

FISHERS OF MEN
Contemporary, faceted glass
Rectangle

Reference B111

ASCENSION
Contemporary, faceted glass
Rectangle

Reference B112

GARDEN OF GETHSEMANE
Contemporary, faceted glass
Rectangle

Reference B113

CROSS SERIES
Traditional African,
faceted glass
Five lancets

Reference B114

MARTIN LUTHER
Contemporary, faceted
Top round, rectangle

Reference B115

SINCE 1971 THE WORK of Ron Bovard has been exhibited at galleries and museums around the world, including the Carnegie Museum of Art. Bovard has had more than twenty-five one-man exhibits. Four of these were at prestigious New York City galleries and three at Vienna, Austria galleries, including his 1984 one-man exhibit at Galerie Kunst Depot during the world famous Vienna Festival. Enthusiastic critiques and reviews of Mr. Bovard's art have been carried in many newspapers and magazines, including The Pittsburgh Press, The New Yorker, and New York's Art Speak. Ron Bovard's artwork has been written about in books published in two languages, distributed in North America and Europe. In addition he has participated in many radio interviews and has been featured in several television programs, including three programs for regional PBS network affiliates.

Some excerpts from what the Critics said about Ron Bovard's Art:

• GREAT ART... "A savvy hayseed...Reminiscent of Grandma Moses...A kissing cousin of that other savvy hayseed Red Grooms" -Art Speak, New York

• ENVIRONMENTAL... "One continuous landscape travels around the four walls of West Broadway" - The New Yorker; "Painting works spatially, communicating a sense of expansion" - Altoona Mirror

• BEAUTY... "...enjoyed for color and design qualities" - Pittsburgh Press; "Rich innocent imagery" - Fairfield Ledger; "His art is pervaded by a peace that is transcendental in nature." - Altoona Mirror

• CONTENT... "This image has the force to counteract our post-industrial fate" - Art Speak, New York; "Simple, charming and innocent" - Ottumwa Courier; "Full of mystery and symbolism" - Pittsburgh Press

• SPIRITUALLY UPLIFTING... "Cosmic" - Pittsburgh Post Gazette; "Represents nature's underlying unmanifest field of being" - Altoona Mirror

SELECTED ONE MAN SHOWS:

• Nov 1987 - Merrill Gallery, Kansas City, MO, USA

• July 1984 - Galerie Flora, Vienna, Austria

• May 1984 - Galerie Kunst Depo, Vienna, Austria

• Sep 1983 - Westbroadway Gallery, New York, NY USA

• Apr 1983 - Lynn Kottler Gallery, New York, NY USA

• Jan 1982 - Alternate Space Gallery, New York, NY USA

• Oct 1980 - Undercroft Gallery, Pittsburgh, PA USA

AUTHOR'S SHOW JOURNAL

CONTACT BOVARD STUDIO

Bovard Studio Inc
2281 Highway 34 East,
Fairfield, IA 52556 USA
Phone: (641) 472-2824
Fax: (641) 472-0974
E-mail: info@bovardstudio.com

WEB SITE ADDRESSES

WINDOWS FOR THE SOUL - WEBSITE
www.windowsforthesoul.com

BOVARD STUDIO - WEBSITE
www.bovardstudio.com

WARDELL PUBLICATIONS - WEBSITE
www.wardellpublications.com

BIBLIOGRAPHY

Note: For more details on sources and resources contained in this book please log onto the book's official web site at: www.windowsforthesoul.com

• Calvet, Jill, "Extreme: Celebrating Superlatives: The Oldest Stained Glass Windows," Ambassador Magazine. Boston and St. Louis: Ambassador Inflight Marketing, January, 1999, p. 20.

• Elskus, Albinas. The Art of Painting on Glass: Techniques and Designs for Stained Glass. New York: Charles Scribner's Sons, 1980.

• Art Business News, Stamford, CT: Myers Publishing Co., Inc. (general source)

• Glass: History, Manufacture and Its Universal Applications. Pittsburgh, Pennsylvania: Pittsburgh Plate Glass Company, 1923.

• Inspired Partnerships, Inc., June 30, 1996. Various authors, Protective Glazing Study for National Preservation Center, Nachitoches, Louisiana. Chicago.

• Sloan, Julie L., "PSG Restoration Report: Protective Glazing." Stained Glass Restoration & Preservation. Published quarterly by Professional Stained Glass magazine –Volume 1, No. 1 – Spring 1990. Brewster, New York: The Edge Publishing Group, Inc.

• Stained Glass Quarterly of the Stained Glass Association of America. Kansas City, Missouri: The Stained Glass Association of America. (general source)

• SGAA Reference & Technical Manual: A Comprehensive Guide To Stained Glass. Kansas City, Missouri: The Stained Glass Association of America, 1992

• Standards and Guidelines for the Preservation of Historic Stained Glass. Kansas City, Missouri: The Stained Glass Association of America, revised November 1998

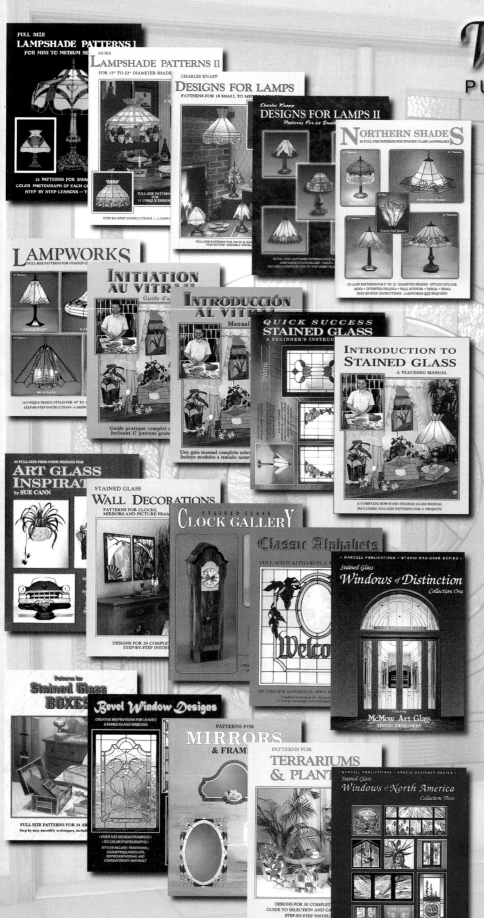

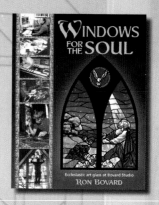
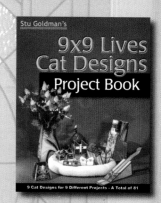
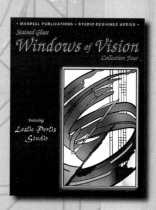
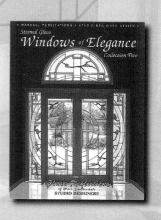